CLEOPATRA AT THE BREAKFAST TABLE

ALSO BY PETER O'BRIEN

Build a Better Book Club
(Macmillan Canada), written with Harry Heft.

Introduction to Literature: British, American, Canadian
(Harper & Row), edited with Robert Lecker and Jack David.

So To Speak: Interviews with Contemporary Canadian Writers
(Véhicule).

Fatal Recurrences: New Fiction in English from Montreal
(Véhicule), edited with Hugh Hood.

Rubicon Literary and Art Journal
(McGill University).

REVIEWS OF AND PRAISE FOR PETER O'BRIEN

"… savvy irreverence … bracing and unexpected combinations, this guide propels us down any number of dream paths we might travel … down-to-earth approach … chatty, accessible tone."

– The Hamilton Spectator

"Book clubs, say the authors of this guidebook, are one of the hot literary trends. … They're right too. … Heft and O'Brien, book-club veterans both, offer a complete inventory, from finding the right mix of people to structuring meetings and inviting guest speakers. An appendix lists 200 thoughtfully chosen works of both fiction and non-fiction to get you going."

– The Globe and Mail

"… electricity, banter, stimulation – call it what you will …"

– Westender

"*Build a Better Book Club* will prove indispensible … helpful advice on a surprising variety of topics."

– www.indigo.ca

"One of the hottest trends … is the book club and the authors offer advice on everything from the books themselves … to creating the right social dynamic among your members."

– The Vancouver Province

"… interesting and informative reading. … the interviewer/letter writer, Peter O'Brien, was well-matched with the authors. … *So To Speak* is, unfortunately, the kind of book too often consigned to library shelves, appreciated by students and not the general reading public. With any luck, though, its worthiness to the average reader will be recognized."

– Marc Côté, The Globe and Mail

"… illuminating in an intellectual way … these interviews are fascinating and immensely valuable for their informal views they give us of creative minds at work."

– George Woodcock, Books in Canada

"A refreshingly random literary tour … The random nature of the book is the most refreshing thing about it. O'Brien's intention was to provide a cross-section of literary voices – male and female, new and old, poet and storyteller – and 'let the traditions fall where they may.' *So To Speak* succeeds in doing that."

– Joel Yanofsky, The Montreal Gazette

"These interviews answer a modern need to add document to creation – a form of oral history … into … writers, their artistic experiments, their strivings, sincerities, postures and endeavours."

– Leon Edel, winner of the National Book Award and Pulitzer Prize

CLEOPATRA
at the BREAKFAST TABLE

Why I Studied Latin
with My Teenager
and How I Discovered
the Daughterland

by PETER O'BRIEN

FOURFRONT EDITIONS

Book and cover composition and design: Julie McNeill, McNeill Design Arts
Cover photograph of "Cleopatra" by Kevin Diamond and Ian Compton, makeup by
Geneviève L'Abbé, pearl-drop earrings by Elaine Wigle Designs, and photo manipulation
by Julie McNeill
Author photograph: Kevin Diamond and Ian Compton
Editor: Allan Briesmaster

Library and Archives Canada Cataloguing in Publication

O'Brien, Peter, 1957-, author
    Cleopatra at the breakfast table : why I studied Latin with my teenager
and how I discovered the daughterland / Peter O'Brien.

Includes index.
ISBN 978-1-927443-66-8 (pbk.)

    1. Fathers and daughters. 2. Interpersonal communication and culture.
3. Education—Effect of technological innovations on. 4. Technological
innovations—Social aspects. 5. Intergenerational relations. 6. Latin
language—Study and teaching. I. Title.

P94.7.O37 2014   302.2   C2014-901064-8

Published by Fourfront Editions
An imprint of Quattro Books Inc.
Toronto
www.quattrobooks.ca

Printed in Canada

For Siobhan

MERITO

CONTENTS

CHAPTER ONE

MY DAUGHTER, ME AND THE MAGISTERIUM

"So what's my dad up to?"
Terence, *The Girl from Andros*

"There's no law against telling the truth with a smile."
Horace, *Satires*

ONCE UPON A RECENT SPRING MORNING my 14-year-old daughter, Siobhan, told me during breakfast that she had settled on her courses for the following school year. One of her electives, she informed me nonchalantly between munches of whole-wheat toast, and sips of cinnamon tea, would be Latin.

As her father, I naturally think that she is beautiful and talented and wise, but I was startled to learn that in our era (consumed with that which it is nourished by: Facebook, YouTube, Twitter and continuous text messaging) Latin was even an option at her local public high school. She had decided, with not an iota of encouragement or pressure from me, to dip her nail-polished toes into the vast and unknown waters of Latin, a language that has been "dead" for 2,000 years or so.

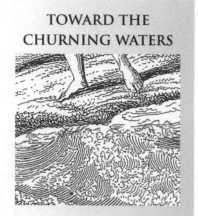

TOWARD THE CHURNING WATERS

When I asked her why she wanted to study an ancient language, she said, in that special tone which teenagers have of talking to their oh-so-out-of-touch parents: "I don't know, Dad. Do I need a reason? I think it will be fun. A bunch of my friends are also taking Latin next year."

Wayfinding for a separated parent with a teenager is, of course, always a challenge. Even with the technological benefit of wireless GPS, accompanied by a standard-issue internal compass, a parent is always on the lookout for unmarked paths and mislabeled routes that must be negotiated. And Siobhan, like all teenagers, has her own distinct vision of the landscape through which she travels, what I've taken to call the Daughterland. One small, cunning example of this. Riding back on the subway from our first trip to her orthodontist, Siobhan looked across at a poster advertising a crisis hotline for kids in trouble. The poster blared:

Thinking of suicide?
There is help.
Let's talk.

and listed a telephone number to call. "Dad," she said, giving me a mischievous jab in the ribs with her elbow, "can you take down that number for me?"

As a former English major who has wandered among books and writers – including a few ancient authors, all in translation, of course – I decided that it might be fun to accompany her on this year-long linguistic adventure, despite the evident navigational hazards. It might help spark my sympathies for this foundational language, might inspire some random reading of a few great writers, and might provide me the opportunity to read about early Roman history and perhaps even consider if there were historical lessons that could be applied to our Internet-infused age. Most important, it might provide me with a way to keep connected, in a fatherly fashion, to Siobhan's expanding teenaged life: the swirling torrents and tumults, the impending serpent's-tooth bouts of "Dad, really! You don't understand anything!" that I thought were sure to be part of her teenaged years.

FATHERLY DAUGHTERLY PLEASURES

"What has nature wanted to be more pleasurable to us, what has nature wanted to be more dear to us, than our daughters."

— Cicero, *In Verrem*

Could I convince her that the two of us studying together wasn't too, using a word she might use, "creepy"? Would I get in her way by being too parentally pedantic? Would I embarrass her (more than I usually do) in front of her friends? Would my language acquisition skills (my grey matter is already turning hard and crusty) be able to keep up with her language acquisition skills (hers is still refreshingly soft and malleable)? Would we still be talking to each other at the end of the school year? I had, as usual, more questions and doubts than answers.

When I asked what she thought of me studying with her (I didn't go into the whole father-daughter bonding stuff), she was initially supportive, I think. "Oh Dad," she said with a bit of a snarky, know-it-all sneer and an upward rolling of the eyes. "Don't you have enough other stuff to do? Aren't you looking for work – you know, paid work? Don't you … ummm, well okay, I guess."

A week later I went back to her. "I'm serious, Scoops," I said. "I'd like to study Latin with you. And that will get me reading some of those old-fart authors I only know a tiny bit about. Who knows? I may be able to read them in the original Latin one day. And I'll get to read about all those curious Roman emperors. And … maybe I'll write a little story about it. I'm not going to class with you! I just want to keep up with your studying and maybe do the same homework."

Realizing that I was rather insistent, she scrunched up her face, rolled those marvelously talented eyes once again (she can make them go seriously cross-eyed, she can roll them up so high that just the white is showing, she can make them cry at will, et cetera) and said to me with all the seriousness she could muster, "Okay, but there are going to be some rules about all this! I don't want you embarrassing me at school! Got it?"

Here is the text that my daughter dictated, that I recorded, and that we both agreed to, by signing and dating the scrap of paper on which it was written:

Restrictions and Rules That My Dad Has to Obey if He Wants to Study Grade 10 Latin With Me

1. You are **not** allowed to come to the class.
2. You are **not** allowed to interview my peers (kids I don't know).
3. You **are** allowed to interview my friends, but only outside of school hours.
4. I would prefer that you not talk with my Latin teacher before the class starts in September.
5. You are allowed to work on this as long as it does not interfere with your real job.

Only with the signing of the agreement "witnessed and attested" by her mother, also known as Sheilagh, also known as my ex-wife (who, it should be noted, was a lawyer and is now a judge), did I think it was safe to proceed. And in my procession I was made to remain acutely appreciative – by both the stern daughter and the legal-minded mother – of the "Thou Shalt Not" flavour of the signed document.

I decided over that first summer, before "our" Latin class started, to acquaint myself with some of the authors who formed such a vast hole in my own education. Virgil, Apuleius, Suetonius, Tacitus, Horace, Ovid, Lucan, Ennius: to me these were just names that I could not really distinguish or differentiate.

As I started to tell a few people about the project, I was intrigued with how many told me that they had studied Latin in high school. Some of them had fond memories about studying the language, while others had entertaining anecdotes to tell. Helen Keeley noted that there were precisely two electives when she was in high school: typing (sure to lead her right to the secretarial pool, she surmised) and Latin (which had some academic gravitas attached to it). She picked Latin, which she studied for the next five years. Helen ended up as an estates and financial planning lawyer. Tom, now a high-tech consultant for multinationals, studied in a one-room schoolhouse, where all the grades were gathered together and all the topics taught by the same person. His teacher was originally from England and had studied Latin. "I was one of only two students in my class who studied Latin, but I enjoyed it, and still recall nuggets of it that our teacher, Mrs. Chichester, instilled in us."

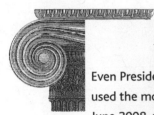

YES WE CAN (SPEAK LATIN)!

Even President Barack Obama invoked (for a time) Latin. He used the motto, "VERO POSSUMUS" ("YES, WE CAN!") in June 2008, and then it was discarded.

And a group of influential conservative pundits, formed after being trounced in the 2012 U.S. presidential election, call themselves Proximus, Latin for "next."

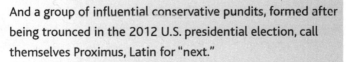

I also spoke with a friend whose mother studied Latin as a young girl in China, I met a young Icelander who had studied Latin in his home country, and I met a woman from Casablanca who studied Latin under her French-language teachers.

Not everyone speaks glowingly of the experience. The great 18th-century writer and dictionary maker Samuel Johnson, when asked by a friend how he came to have such an accurate knowledge of Latin, spoke of his teacher at the Lichfield Grammar School who "whipt me very well.

ROOTS

It is fascinating to consider the multitude of ideas and elements of our language that have Latin, and sometimes Greek, at their root. Common words and concepts such as education, democracy, history, pleasure and pain all derive from Latin roots. In addition, don't ignore words such as television, Wikipedia, Facebook, text message, YouTube, Internet and computer – all these words have their genesis in Latin! It is accurate to say that English, and various other languages, are abundantly influenced by Latin, and by studying Latin we have a more complete understanding of English.

(Here, to prove the point, are the words from the above paragraph that have their full or partial roots in Latin.)

fascinating from L. fascinatus, the past participle (pp.) of fascinare "bewitch, enchant, fascinate"

consider from L. considerare "to look at closely, observe"

multitude from L. multitudinem "a great number, crowd"

idea from L. idea "idea"

elements from L. elementem "rudiment, first principle, matter in its most basic form"

language from L. lingua "tongue," also "speech, language"

root connected with the L. radix

common from late 14c. L. communis served as a noun meaning "common property, state, commonwealth"

concepts from Middle L. conceptum "draft, abstract"; in classical Latin "(a thing) conceived"

education from L. educatus, pp. of educare "bring up, rear, educate," which is related to educere "bring out, lead forth"

democracy from the Greek, then L. democratia "democracy"

history from L. historia "narrative, account, tale, story"

pleasure from L. placeo "be pleasing," "satisfy"

pain from L. poena "punishment, penalty"

derive from L. derivare "to lead or draw off (a stream of water) from its source"

addition from L. additionem "an adding to, addition"

ignore from L. ignorare "not to know, disregard," from ignarus "not knowing, unaware"

Wikipedia wiki – a technology for creating collaborative websites, from the Hawaiian word "wiki" meaning "quick"; encyclopedia: from the L., taken as "general education," but literally "training in a circle," i.e. the "circle" of arts and sciences

television tele from Greek. tele-, combining form of tele "far off, afar, at or to a distance," related to teleos "end, goal, result, consummation, perfection," literally "completion of a cycle"; vision from L. visionem "act of seeing, sight, thing seen," from a stem of videre "to see"

face from L. facies "appearance, form, figure"

text from L. textus "style or texture of a work"

message from L. missus, pp. of mittere "to send"

YouTube You from L. tu; Tube from L. tubus "tube, pipe," of unknown origin

Internet inter from L., literally "amongst other things" (the Latin for "among other persons" is inter alios); net from L. nodus "knot"

computer from L. computare "to count, sum up, reckon together"

genesis from L. genesis, adopted as title of first book of the Old Testament in Vulgate, from Greek genesis "origin, creation, generation"

accurate from L. accuratus "prepared with care, exact, elaborate"

say from Old L. inseque "to tell, say"

English from L. Angli "the Angles," literally "people of Angul"

various from L. varius "changing, different, diverse"

other from L. alter, from base al- "beyond" plus -tero "second"

abundantly from L. abundantem "overflowing"

influenced from L. influentem "to flow into," from in "in" plus fluere "to flow"

studying from L. studium "study, application," originally "eagerness," from studere "to be diligent"

complete from L. completus, "to fill up, complete the number of (a legion, etc.)," transferred to "to fill, to fulfill, to finish (a task)"

understand from L. inter "between, among"; from L. stare "stand"

And in case you are wondering, the words "it," "is," "to," "the," "of," "a," "that," "or," "as," "in," "at," "by," "from" and "and" also have been influenced by or come directly to us from Latin. And just one more word from the above paragraph: the word "Latin" comes from the Latin word Latinus or "belonging to Latium," the region of Italy around Rome. (The word "paragraph" also, of course, comes to us from the Latin, but this endless etymology is now starting to get out of hand! Yikes – "etymology" also comes to us from Latin!) As a mathematician or lawyer might say: QED (quod erat demonstrandum, which means "that which was to be demonstrated or proven").

Without that, Sir, I should have done nothing." One of the people I interviewed for this book, James Morwood, the editor of the *Pocket Oxford Latin Dictionary* and many other books, noted: "one of my teachers used to hit me over the head with a big Latin dictionary when I made a bad mistake" and he mentioned that "a former and fairly bald colleague told me that he had a hair pulled out each time he made a bad mistake!"

I assumed that teachers didn't still spend their time whipping, hitting and plucking students to assist in the learning of the language, but I wasn't quite sure that Latin was even teachable or learnable without such incentives. I started to wade into the first shallow waters of actually learning a few words of the language, by going online and making use of various dictionaries and translation guides, and by purchasing a few books with such titles as *Introductory Latin* and *Hey Old Man, Don't You Think You Are Too Old To Start Studying an Ancient Language?*

I learned, much to my pleasure, that many of the English words that my daughter and I already spoke – perhaps as high as 60 percent – had come to us from Latin, either as the language began to flourish in the last few centuries BCE, or as it was later adapted by the Roman Catholic Church and Chaucer, Shakespeare and Dryden over the years. So I could say, sort of, that I was already a 60-percent Latin speaker.

All of this activity – the reading, interviews and specks of research I was doing – I tried to keep secret from my daughter, fearing that if she knew the amount of attention I was giving this, she would react, well, with some teenaged "concern" for my mental wellbeing. That she refers to her mother and me as "the mental parentals" is just the sort of standard operating procedure that most parents deal with on a daily basis.

Whenever she caught me trying to stifle my delight at discovering a connection between our era and that of Romans (reading about Angelina Jolie seeking a director for her new movie about Cleopatra, noting Anthony Bourdain's tweet comparing Toronto mayor Rob Ford to Caligula), I made sure not to make anything too big out of it. I'd merely ask her: "You're still okay with me doing this, aren't you, Sweetie-Poopsie-Darling-Angel-From-Heaven?" Her response was often a non-committal grunt, and sometimes a lash of ironic humour: "Oh Dad, I forgot to tell you. I'm not doing Latin anymore – I decided to switch to Spanish!"

Once, when I wondered out loud whether I could get a copy of the Latin textbook "we" were going to be using that coming September, she said: "Oh, Dad, please don't talk to my teacher – he's going to tell the whole class that you're doing this. Mortifying, Dad. It's just mortifying!" I was able to remind her that, according to our signed agreement, I was fully within my rights to talk to "our" teacher, at least once September arrived. Even her mother had a definitive response to this idea of contacting the teacher before I was contractually permitted to do so: "Excuse me, but you two have a signed agreement," she said, giving me the no-nonsense judge-look that she must use in the courtroom. "If you want an amendment to the agreement, then that has to be negotiated and a new amended agreement has to be drawn up." Yikes! All I wanted to do was get a bit of head-start on my studying!

In the midst of this preliminary research, I thought it might be clever, linguistically speaking, to find a Roman Catholic Church that still did its service in Latin – it being one of the main institutions still marinating in Latin. I was delighted to discover, for example, that one of the eight languages of the Vatican's website was Latin (alongside Chinese, Dutch, English, French, Italian, Portuguese and Spanish).

As an altar boy in Vancouver in the 1960s I had learned the standard Latin responses that I needed to know by rote, without any understanding of their meaning. Now I can only dimly remember two nonsensical conflations of Latin and English: "ekum

SACRED LATIN

From the Latin page of the Vatican's website.

spirit two-two-oh" (which most altar boys remember as the telephone number for heaven!) and "dominus vobiscum" – (in my mind always connected to Nabisco Shredded Wheat cereal). Perhaps by attending a Latin mass, went my reasoning, I'll be able to clarify these linguistic black holes.

I attended, it must be said, a good many Catholic services over the years: every Sunday as a kid, as a result of attending nothing but Catholic schools up to and including my first university degree (I started Grade 1 at a school called Immaculate Conception and graduated with a BA from the University of Notre Dame) and by way of a couple of church marriages in which I had an important role. I learned about extreme unction and transubstantiation but nothing about the linguistic roots of the Catholic Church. Unlike James Joyce, who was saturated with ecclesiastical Latin (and then famously declares, *"Non Serviam"* – "I will not serve" – in *A Portrait of the Artist as a Young Man*), I was not obligated to study the language. And unlike international singer and songwriter Gordon Lightfoot, who studied Latin at Orillia District Collegiate and Vocational Institute in the 1950s, I was never given the option to study Latin, even if I wanted to. "I had the same teacher for both music and Latin," Gordon told me. "My Latin class was the first of the day and I really had to fight to stay awake … My teacher wasn't really the right one to teach Latin – he couldn't inspire the students. But with music he was much better."

For my BA at Notre Dame I had to take credit courses in science, mathematics and philosophy, and even had to pass a swimming test, but was never required to study Latin.

There was no dogmatic or overtly religious reason why I had attended Catholic schools. Of my voluminous family – the immediate family is a conglomeration of three brothers, six sisters, eight step-brothers and four step-sisters (for a grand total of 22) – I was the only one to do so. No nudging from my mother, although I do remember how she introduced me to some of her friends: "Here is Peter. He is an altar boy now, and later he'll be a priest, and then a bishop, and then a cardinal, and then the Pope!"

I didn't live up to my Mom's expectations.

Despite the fact that I never became Pope I guess there remains some faint draught of clerical incense still swirling around in my lungs.

But in my search for ancient things such as a Catholic mass in Latin, the Internet is, indeed, a marvelous tool. With one click I had what I was looking for: the local Traditional Mass Society. The society, said the website, "is a registered chapter of the International Una Voce Federation. We are an association of lay Catholics in the Archdiocese of Toronto, loyal to the Magisterium and hierarchy of the Catholic Church." I learned that within a short drive of my apartment, there were six churches that offered masses in Latin. One church offering a sung mass in Latin was a 15-minute walk away.

Over the course of the summer I was to become, to some minimal degree at least, loyal to the "Magisterium." I wasn't really sure what the "Magisterium" was, but it certainly sounded impressive, and I thought it would be something I could perhaps use to my advantage. I imagined Siobhan saying to me: "Dad, I don't really want to clean up my room," to which I would respond, with deepened voice, compressed eyebrows, and a sombre but pontifical wave of the hand: "I will have you know, young lady, that I am loyal to the Magisterium and you will now commence to clean your room and on this point of honour related to abstersion and lixiviation [I had found a couple of great Latinate synonyms related to cleaning that I was sure would impress her] I am, it is not inaccurate to say, quite steadfastly committed!"

So the summer before "our" class started, I attended Latin mass a couple of times. I was ecstatic (well perhaps that is a bit much – I'm no Saint Theresa) when I could pick out a few words, worn down and covered with dust, but not obliterated, by non-use:

In nomine Patris et Filii et Spiritus Sancti.
In the name of the Father and of the Son and of the Holy Spirit.

Mea culpa, mea culpa, mea máxima culpa.
My bad, my bad, my really bad.

And I was able to correct and clarify my earlier mistaken Latin: "*Dominus vobiscum*" means, in English: "The Lord be with you," which is followed in the service of the mass not by "Ekum spirit two-two-oh" but more properly by *"et cum spirit tuo"* which means "And also with you." Okay, I was starting to connect some linguistic dots.

My other great find that summer was Elaine Fantham. In my background reading and Internet scouring, I kept coming across her name and her writings. A former named professor at Princeton University, Elaine, as one of her colleagues says, is "the *grande dame* of Latin studies in the English-speaking world." I finally decided that I should contact her and see if she would be willing to answer a few emailed questions about this quixotic idea I had of studying Latin with my daughter.

VOCABULARY LESSON

begin – v. initium facio
book – n. liber
daughter – n. filia
father – n. pater
question – n. interrogatio; v. interrogo

PRACTICING THE LANGUAGE

Because of a daughter, a father starts studying Latin.
Filiae causa pater incipit linguam Latinam discere.

I discovered that she had retired from Princeton in 2000, and that she now had her own website. I read that she had taught earlier in her career, and post-retirement, at the University of Toronto. And then that she was currently living in Toronto. And then – who knows whether it was seren-dipity or fortuna or fate – that she lived across the street from me! I could see her building from my building.

At first Elaine seemed bemused about my naïve and formless interest in studying Latin, but she was quite willing to assist the process by loan-ing me books and magazine articles. We also started going to see a few plays and movies together, including the full, uncut version of *Spartacus* and Woody Allen's *To Rome With Love*. And we started enjoying together a small tradition that continues – imbibing in the sweet and smoky pleasures of single malt, including Lagavulin and Dalwhinnie.

In preparation for the year's course of study, and with Elaine's encour-agement, I began reading a few Roman authors, in English of course. The only proviso was that the writers had to be entertaining. As soon as I got bored, or thought that the writer wasn't providing enough humour or insight, I abandoned the book and moved on to something else. I really did have rather low expectations – entertain me or I'm moving on!

In my existing speck of wisdom about the Latin authors, I'd always been surprised that – sprinkled among the great philosophical wisdoms and the mythological foundations of their writing – they are just as pruri-ent, immature, silly and petty as anyone else I've ever known or anyone else I've ever read. And virtually no topic is off limits. I was now having the opportunity to prove the rudimentary conclusions I had come to.

There is, of course, insight about the origins of the universe (in Lucretius and Ovid) and about matters spiritual and rational (Virgil, Marcus Aurelius) and about matters historical and political (Tacitus, Pliny). But there are also other universes of matters that are truly spicy and provocative, and perhaps not necessarily appropriate for teenage consump-tion. Throughout Apuleius, Horace, Martial and Catullus there is garden-variety heterosexual lust and sex, as well as many other variations (mas-turbation, homosexuality, incest, necrophilia, bestiality, cross-dressing, a talking penis, what is now known on TV ads as "Erectile Dysfunction," et cetera, sometimes very graphically presented).

There are also discourses on bad breath and poor dental hygiene in Petronius and Seneca, although my favourite is probably in Catullus, where he talks about a Spaniard who hoards his "night piss" and then uses it the next morning to "scrub off his teeth, *and* his sore red gums."

There are discourses on drunkenness and the carousing that results, with one of my favourites being in the Plautus play *The Brothers Menaechmus,* where one of the characters talks about the wild and unexpected joys he's had that day: "I've wined, I've dined, I've concubined," and when another character, holding up a woman's dress that he's stolen, asks a friend to describe what he smells, the friend says "purloin, sirloin and her loin."

And discourses on the power of rumour and gossip (not a surprise, considering that one of the Roman gods was Fama, the God of Rumour). And on gambling, with Juvenal in the *Satires* speaking of his age as though he is talking about ours: "When has gambling been more frantic / Than it is today?"

There are some marvelous insults: "You ruin the bath by rinsing your rear end in it, but if you really want to insult it, stick your head in it." (Martial); "Ex-tenant of a pigsty." (Cicero); and "Low-life trapeze-artist!" (Juvenal). And there are discussions of female mud-wrestling, speed-eating contests, talk of the constant and desperate search for money, a continuous rumble of distaste and regret for the obsession over fashion, hairstyles, and excessive jewellery, and all manner of what Samuel Johnson called, in his translation of Juvenal's tenth satire, "the vanity of human wishes."

In brief – what's not to love about these writers?

With these unconnected snippets of knowledge, these loose threads that my daughter helped present to me and that I then started to weave together, I set out on this journey toward Latin and its partially sunken treasures. In the opening address to the reader in *The Golden Ass*, often credited as the first novel ever written, and certainly one of the sauciest, Apuleius says: *"Lector intende: laetaberis"* ("Reader, pay attention: you will enjoy yourself"). I thought that if I could pay attention to my Latin studies, do all the homework that Siobhan was assigned, and keep up my reading of these classical writers, I would enjoy myself. Or at least that was the intent.

CHAPTER TWO

LATIN, LATIN EVERYWHERE

"Latin is the commander of all languages."
Honorius of Autun, *Gemma Animae*

"His mind is one vast wasteland."
Sallust, *Bellum Catilinae*

O N THE DOORWAY LEADING INTO Siobhan's Latin classroom, which also ended up functioning as her Grade 10 homeroom, are the words: "Latin isn't dead. It just changed its name."

I knew of this phrase earlier because, despite the standing "legal" agreement that had been drawn up, I did circumvent "Restriction and Rule Number 4." I decided to contact "our" Latin teacher, Matthew Skinner, in June, before her Grade 9 school year had ended and the summer had begun. If I was going to get my Latin-acquisition skills in shape (I surreptitiously reasoned) then I needed to have the textbooks in hand as soon as I could. When I told Matthew about my plans to study Latin with my daughter, he was both enthusiastic and accommodating. He arranged for the two textbooks to be left at the main school office, and when I went to pick them up I took a quick peek at the main Latin classroom. Matthew also told me about an end-of-year classics conference for high school students. "The conference is a lot of fun. For some students, that's the highlight of the school year," he said. "It'll be happening in May and it might be something you want to go to."

LATIN IS CRESTING AT SIOBHAN'S HIGH SCHOOL

The back cover of Siobhan's high school yearbook. The crest of Humberside Collegiate Institute, established in 1892, includes the Latin motto, "FELIX QUI POTUIT RERUM COGNOSCERE CAUSAS" which is translated by the school as "Happy is the person who has been able to learn the reasons of things."

I immediately imagined myself at the conference (not unlike some of the conferences I had attended when I was a high school student) wandering among the cardboard displays on Latin grammar, attending a few talks about Roman gladiatorial contests or the gossipy graffiti left on the walls of Pompeii, and sharing funny stories with my fellow students. I thought that there was no reason a parent would feel at all out of place in such a gathering. "High school confidential" and "adult confidential": there didn't seem much of a difference to me.

I cannot say, at first glance, that the Latin textbooks Siobhan and I are using, the *Cambridge Latin Course* (or the *CLC*, as they are better known), are daunting books. There is no diving into the bracing, dark depths of Latin. Throughout the books there is lots of English, as well as plentiful drawings and photographs. The linguistic ramp up to "Verbs with the Dative," "Subordinate Conjunctions" and the 1st, 2nd, 3rd, 4th and 5th declensions is very gradual.

The books begin by describing the daily adventures of a typical nuclear family in 1st-century Pompeii. The father, Lucius Caecilius Iucundus (Iucundus means "pleasant," we are told), the mother Metella (one of whose tasks was to supervise the "work of domestic slaves"), and the son Quintus, who is about 15 years of age, spend their days studying, reading, going to the market, the baths, the forum or the gladiatorial shows, or playing with the dog, Cerberus.

In the hopes that it might provide me with some Latinate inspiration, I also joined the "We Love Quintus" Facebook fan page. It ended up being a forum for a bunch of high school kids to talk about their teachers and exchange a few snippets of gossip, and not so much about the *CLC* or learning Latin. In a typical posting, one of the girls who helped set up the fan page provides an insight into her newly found romantic guidepost: "Now that I do Latin, I compare every guy I meet to Quintus," she said. I left the site not long after I joined it, thinking that hanging around on a teenage fan page – even one devoted to my new Latin textbook – might be, to use that word again, a bit creepy.

QUINTUS HAS HIS OWN FACEBOOK FAN PAGE

Quintus holding the Cambridge Latin Course textbook from the Facebook fan page "We Love Quintus."

Although I studied and learned some rudimentary French over the years, and actually won the Grade 10 Spanish contest at my high school, Vancouver College, with the phrase "Mi casa es amarillo, verde y azul," I am not what could be called a natural or intuitive language learner. The *CLC*, with its gentle, hand-holding tone – "Metella was very fond of jewellery. Here are some samples of the things she might have worn." – is about at the right level for me.

Precisely because of this we-hope-we're-not-going-too-fast-for-you tone, the *CLC* is not universally lauded, especially among the hard-core Latin students of an earlier age. Harry Mount, who wrote *Amo, Amas, Amat*, which has helped popularize and encourage the study of Latin, is dismissive of the *CLC*. Mount states rather angrily: "Death to the Cambridge Latin Course." He refers to it as "the evil Latin-for-dummies" textbook "used in

80 percent of schools which offer Latin." Mount, of course, studied Latin the old-fashioned way: by learning how to recognize the passive periphrastic when he saw it, and by knowing enough of the inflected vocabulary that he could translate previously unseen chunks of Cicero in class.

But for me, trying to wander through the darkened labyrinthine hallways of a new language? I'm just happy in these early days in being able to dine on a few sweet and familiar morsels that I already know: *modus operandi, post mortem,* and then add a few more simple words about Caecilius, Metella and Quintus – words such as *hortus* (garden), *cubiculum* (bedroom), *culina* (kitchen) and *canis* (dog).

Of note in the *CLC* is the lack of female characters, and in my readings of the classical texts there is a notable lack of female authors. In the paternalistic society of classical Rome, where the fathers had ultimate power over education, life and death, this should not really be much of a surprise, and yet it is to me. As Elaine Fantham says in *Roman Literary Culture,* "the author in Roman culture is usually, however regrettably, male." Other than Sappho (who wrote in Greek) the only female author from classical times that I've come across is Sulpicia, and there are only six poems in Latin of hers which survive.

The short poems that Sulpicia wrote to her lover, Cerinthus, are rather slight commentaries on missing him and on being bored with life in the country:

> My birthday's arrived and I hate it –
> of all days to be spent in the gloom
> and boredom of the country
> without Cerinthus!
> Where is life sweeter than in the city?

Sounds to me like the typical regrets of the average teenager, hankering after things that are deliciously new and lamentably unattainable.

I wonder if the paternalism for which the Roman Empire and Latin is so well-known will develop in Siobhan a less-than-enthusiastic affection for the language, a feeling from her of "How could they have been so dumb, so small-minded, so dismissive about women?" but I decide to stifle those concerns and let her come to such conclusions, or not, on her own.

The few other female writers in Latin who have come down to us from the past include Hildegard von Bingen (1098–1179), the head of her German convent, who travelled widely on preaching tours, wrote about her visions which she had when she was "awake and alert and with a clear mind," composed music, and even created her own alphabet, a sort of improvised Medieval Latin that she called *Lingua Ignota* (Latin for "unknown language"). There is some debate as to whether Hildegard intended her constructed language to be a new universal language or whether she had created it just for the nuns in her abbey, not unlike those who created the Klingon language for *Star Trek*, the Dothraki language for use in *Game of Thrones*, or the Na'vi language for the large blue residents of Pandora in James Cameron's movie *Avatar*. Perhaps Hildegard created the language exclusively for her own private use. We just don't know.

HILDEGARD VON BINGEN'S SECRET LANGUAGE

Another nun, Hrotsvitha von Gandersheim (c. 935 – c. 1002), generally acknowledged as the first female playwright, wrote Latin comedies in the style of Terence. In one, *Dulcitius*, a randy prefect who is hoping to enjoy the pleasures of three virgins instead ends up caressing and cavorting with kitchen pots and pans, much to the amusement and disdain of his attendants and his wife.

I am pleased that Hrotsvitha continues to have some resonance in our own day. Recently, the American feminist performance and drama group Guerrilla Girls on Tour! – an offshoot of the original Guerrilla Girls – issued on their website the "Hrotsvitha Challenge." The Hrotsvitha Award is to be given to a professional theatre that had decided to "scrap their plans

of producing yet another production of a Greek tragedy and instead pro-
duce a play by Hrotsvitha."

In the midst of these first feeble attempts at studying classical Latin and
reading about the Romans, I am seeing the language and its influence
everywhere around me. It's similar to when you get a new pair of glasses or
a new haircut: for the next day or so all you seem to notice is other people's
glasses or the hairstyles on everyone you pass on the street. Self-centred
and perhaps self-indulgent, it is also a sign that we are usually so ignorant
or unaware of our immediate surroundings and the tinctured colours and
whimsical shapes that our daily lives present to us. To highlight just a few
examples of how often I noted the influence of my new fixation:

❀ Wandering around the TV late one evening, I stumble upon a
scene from *Young Man with a Horn,* a film based on the life of Bix
Beiderbecke, starring Lauren Bacall and Kirk Douglas. At one point
Bacall approaches Douglas, and takes the trumpet out of his hand:

> Bacall: Let's put your "alter ego" away.
> Douglas: My what?!
> Bacall: Latin. A dead language that ideally suits me. It simply
> means "your other self."

❀ In *The Nun's Story*, Audrey Hepburn speaks, prays and sings in Latin.

❀ For the 10th anniversary of the 9/11 attacks on New York, the Ground
Zero planning committee chose a few translated words from Virgil's
Aeneid to memorialize the victims of that tragic day: "No day shall
erase you from the memory of time" is now a permanent statement
formed into the concrete of the memorial.

❀ Wandering around the Internet I note that even Dana White, the guru of
the mixed martial arts organization Ultimate Fighting Championship
(UFC), surely one of the closest "sports" that our generation has to
the bloody spectacle of Roman gladiatorial contests, invokes Latin. For

the weigh-in of UFC 131 in Vancouver, White wore a T-shirt with the words VERITAS AEQUITAS emblazoned on it. I'm not sure if White ever studied Latin, but he certainly has no trouble celebrating the language. By the way, *veritas aequitas* (made popular by the tattoos on the heroic brothers in the movie *The Boondock Saints*) means "truth and justice."

❁ I walk down a residential side-street in the "Little Italy" neighbourhood of Toronto heading for dinner one evening and come upon a concrete façade sculpture of a Roman chariot race.

❁ Latin and invocations of the Roman Empire are everywhere in classic and current Hollywood flicks as well: in *Little Fockers*, the family motto of Jack Byrnes (Robert De Niro) is in Latin; one of

A LOCAL CHARIOT RACE

A Roman chariot race, as seen in our local "Little Italy."

George Clooney's recent movies is *The Ides of March*; Channing Tatum and Donald Sutherland star in *The Eagle*, about the last days of the Roman Empire; in *Girls*, the TV show created by and starring Lena Dunham, the homeless Ray is taking a PhD in "Latin Studies"; and like Elizabeth Taylor and Vivien Leigh before her, Angelina Jolie is set to play the iconic and much-maligned Cleopatra in an upcoming movie, presumably with Brad Pitt playing Mark Antony. (Okay, maybe not "everywhere" or in "every" Hollywood movie, but certainly there are enough allusions and enough reliance on material passed on to us from those Roman times to keep my antenna tingling.)

❁ Of course Latin is omnipresent in books. It is there on every page of James Joyce's masterwork *Finnegans Wake*. It is a significant pivot point in one of my all-time favourite contemporary novels, Cormac McCarthy's *Blood Meridian*: "Then about the meridian of that day we came upon the judge … He had with him that selfsame rifle you see with him now, all mounted in german silver and the name that he'd give it set with silver wire under the checkpiece in latin: *Et In Arcadio Ego*. A reference to the lethal in it." It is a central note of defiance in Margaret Atwood's novel *The Handmaid's Tale,* as the handmaid Offred discovers a Latin inscription carved into the wood of her small room by the previous handmaid: *Nolitete bastardes carborundorum* (Don't let the bastards grind you down). And throughout Suzanne Collins' book *The Hunger Games,* where we find the nation of Panem (see Juvenal, *panem et circenses* / bread and circuses), and characters such as Cinna, Cato, Flavius, Octavia and Portia. And of course in the Harry Potter books, where Harry seems always to be spouting Latinesque spells (J. K. Rowling studied Latin). Et cetera.

❀ And then there is the use of the "Latin" holiday term "Festivus." First used in a 1997 *Seinfeld* show, the term is used by Siobhan's school as the name of their school-wide December holiday gathering. The term "Festivus Maximus" was also put to good use by the NFL's Baltimore Ravens in 2000, and it may very well have helped them win Super Bowl XXXV (note the Roman numerals) against the New York Jets that year. The Ravens' coach, Brian Billick, wanted his players to concentrate on every game and so banned the words "playoffs" – the players instead used the word "Festivus" for "playoffs" and the words "Festivus Maximus" for the "Super Bowl."

❀ And then there is Bob Dylan using translations of Ovid done by noted Latin translator Peter Green for song lyrics on his albums *Love and Theft* (2001) and *Modern Times* (2006).

❀ I read that there is a Finnish radio station that broadcasts a weekly news summary, *"Nuntii Latini,"* in Latin, and that there is a Finnish university professor who performs several songs by Elvis Presley in Latin. "Quate, Crepa, Rota" ("Shake, Rattle and Roll") anyone?

❀ And Beyoncé gets a horsefly named after her by Bryan Lessard, a researcher at the Australian National Insect Collection. "It was the unique dense golden hairs on the fly's abdomen that led me to name this fly in honour of the performer," Lessard said. In a moment of entomological enthusiasm, he referred to the fly being "bootylicious," but also made sure to note the fly's full name, in Latin of course (all such classifications are in Latin): *Scaptia (plinthina) beyonceae.*

❀ The woman who sold me my Starbucks coffee, Luciana, studied Latin in Italy; my optometrist, Dragana, studied Latin in Serbia; my postie, Theresa, studied Latin in Canada; a woman I worked with at The Leo Baeck Day School, Linda, studied Latin in South Africa; and … well you get the idea how I started to see Latin everywhere.

I try not to express my excitement to Siobhan each time I see a reference to Latin and the Roman Empire, but it is difficult.

About the only place I am not witnessing Latin everywhere is in my own "studying" of the language. Like some high school students, I am less than industrious, less than committed to my homework assignments. Sure, I am talking with a lot of people who studied Latin, and I'm reading the classical authors in English, but the fact remains that I am not really studying Latin in any serious way. I blame all this on Siobhan. She is, in her typical fashion, not sharing with me every detail of her life, every pathway and every switchback that she encounters along the way. I keep having to ask her about the Latin quizzes, and trying to make sure that I know what vocabulary and what grammar she is studying:

"Um, Dad, do I really have to tell you everything about the class? Everything about upcoming quizzes and tests? Everything about what every single student is doing each and every class?"

To which I respond, of course, "Yes. How else am I going to keep up, Siobhannie? How else am I really going to get the feeling of what it's like to be in the classroom, studying next to you? How else am I going to learn Latin?"

"Dad, really, I have other homework to do. And I have to practice piano. Oh, what are we having for supper tonight? And don't forget to sign those papers for my field trip tomorrow. Okay … I have to study now … can you please leave me alone? Umm … Thank you!"

A FATHER IN HIS ATRIUM

Try as I might, I wasn't really being fully welcomed into the typical life of a teenaged high school student. I wasn't even aware of Siobhan's first Latin vocabulary quiz until after it had happened. She got 24 out of 25, I'm happy to say, but I still wish I had known about it before getting a rather perfunctory report on it after the fact. "Oh Dad, I had a quiz yesterday," she mumbled over dinner one evening. "We marked it in class right away. I did okay." I

The first drawing Siobhan did for her Latin class – a certain fatherly bobblehead in his atrium.

tried to remind her that I was not just a curious onlooker – that I am in fact an active participant in all this, but she seemed to barely absorb my hankering comments. So much for studying with or alongside her … so much for daughterly wisdom passed on to a fatherly presence …

Midway through the third week of the school year, Humberside Collegiate had its curriculum night, and Siobhan's mother and I both attended. At least this would give me a chance to get closer to the action, or so I thought.

Matthew, the Latin teacher, was very welcoming to the parents. He noted that although there aren't many Latin programs these days, where they do exist, they are thriving. For the current academic year, he noted that Humberside had 94 Grade 10 students studying Latin, 34 Grade 11 students, and 24 Grade 12 students. Impressive numbers. Here we are in the "Era of Facebook," and 94 out of Siobhan's 250 fellow Grade 10 students had chosen to study Latin. Matthew noted that in Grade 10 the emphasis was more on grammar and vocabulary, but that by Grade 12 the students were expected to be able to translate a chunk of Virgil's *Aeneid* on their own.

VOCABULARY LESSON

everywhere – adv. ubique

money – n. pecunia

school – n. schola

see – v. video

teacher – n. magister

PRACTICING THE LANGUAGE

I am beginning to see the Latin language everywhere.
Incipio verba Latina passim et ubique conspicere.

After the curriculum night, I tried to get out in front of Siobhan's second Latin quiz. The day before her quiz I must have expressed some concern (ill-founded, as usual) as to whether she had been studying sufficiently. I also noted that even though it was "our" class, I would not be there to take the test with her, or even alongside her. Her response: "Oh, I guess that's right, Dad, you can't take the test – so does that mean if I fail, then you also fail!?" (She seems to have found an edge of biting humour somewhere, although I can't quite figure out where it came from.) I did ask her if I could at least quiz her on the words she needed to know, and she thought that was not such a bad idea. Among the words:

atrium – atrium
iratus – angry
tablinum – study
scribit – he/she writes
animus – life
dormit – he/she sleeps
pestis – pest

I was not too much of a *pestis* during our study session, and I certainly didn't get *iratus* when she got a word wrong. Trying to memorize the same words at the same time, I note how much faster Siobhan is at absorbing them than I am. As a teenager I could absorb a few lines of poetry pretty easily, and there are some lines that I can still recall at will, but now it takes me much longer to memorize new words and new phrases, and it is, I have to say, frustrating.

To placate my own feelings of inadequacy, I decided to make a list of some Latin words I already knew. Although English is not directly derived from Latin – it is not one of the Romance languages – it still has an enormous number of words that come from Latin. So here are some Latin words that I already knew:

addendum	*decorum*	*ipso facto*	*percent*
ad nauseam	*ex libris*	*mania*	*referendum*
bona fide	*gymnasium*	*non sequitur*	*translator*
carpe diem	*hyphen*	*panacea*	*verbatim*

In addition to my personal favourite: *et cetera*. This gave me some comfort, because at least I knew many more words of Latin than, for example, Chinese or Japanese or Urdu or Bantu or any other of the hundreds of other languages out there. And if I ever lament how little Latin I know, or how it seems to be forgotten these days, I can always pull out a coin or a dollar bill and read some Latin.

So I have the *CLC* on my bookcase and I spend a few moments here and there feeling smug about Latin words that I've known for decades. And what does it mean, really, that Latin is everywhere around us? What does it mean that we live within the influence of Latin, both consciously and unconsciously? That it informs our democracies, our legal systems, medicine, law, science? That it is embroidered into the fabric of our language – itself always being reformed and augmented and diminished? Who cares that, if we choose to watch out for it, we will see its fingerprints everywhere? Does knowing that Latin is a foundation of our civilization (both high culture and low culture) make our lives richer, better, more colourful?

Of course, I have no good answers for these questions. Perhaps the language itself, or the mere act of attempting to learn the language, as well as a bit about the geography and culture that spawned it, will provide some answers. But whatever the unfelt and unrecognized effects of the language are, however these questions are posed or answered, I am beginning to see the

SHOW ME THE LATIN!

Latin is everywhere on our money. Here, from the U.S. dollar bill:

ANNUIT COEPTIS: Providence Has Favored Our Undertakings

NOVUS ORDO SECLORUM: A New Order of the Ages

And don't forget the Roman numerals MDCCLXXVI, for the year 1776.

Elsewhere on the bill are the words *E PLURIBUS UNUM* (Out of Many, One), so that makes four elements of Latin on the bill!

And on the Canadian quarter: *Dei Gratia Regina* is often abbreviated as *D. G. Regina*: By the Grace of God, Queen.

Early American paper money:

Four shillings & sixpence / Issued in defence of American Liberty / Ense petit placidam sub Libertate Quietem / December 7, 1775 – the Latin phrase can be translated as "by the sword we seek peace, but peace only under liberty."

And a coin issued during the time of the Emperor Domitian:

The letters that encircle the image of Domitian:

CAESAR DIVI F[elix] DOMITIANVS CO[n] S[vl] VII.

world, for better or ill, through Latin-tinted glasses.

The word "money" itself is derived from the Latin *moneta*, meaning "mint" or "coinage," from Moneta, a title of the Roman goddess Juno, protector of funds, in whose temple money was coined. It may, according to etymologists, also come from the word *monere*: "advise, warn."

And one more question about money: does it stink or not? The phrase *pecunia non olet* ("money does not stink") is ascribed to the Emperor Vespasian. When he imposed a Urine Tax – at the time urine from the public urinals was used in tanning and by launderers as a source of ammonia to clean and whiten togas – his son Titus criticized him. Vespasian, according to Suetonius, "held up a coin from the first payment to his son's nose and asked him if he was offended by the smell."

CHAPTER THREE

FROM LIVY (140+ BOOKS) TO TWITTER (140– CHARACTERS)

"Manifold amusements have led to people's obsession
with ruining themselves."
Livy, *The Rise of Rome*

"No sooner does each thing enter our sight than it has been swept away."
Marcus Aurelius, *Meditations*

IS THE INTERNET MAKING US STUPID? Is our access to unlimited information negating our natural ability and instinct to remember? Is our addiction to games and other forms of screen-based entertainment leading to stunted brains? (The Kaiser Family Foundation recently reported that American children and teenagers spend almost eight hours a day in front of screens! And Salar Kamangar, the CEO of YouTube, is convinced that "screen time in general will increase" in the coming years.) Is our reliance on the word-crumbs encouraged by text messaging and Twitter slowly eating away, byte by byte, at our intelligence, our wit, our imagination?

I have to say that I'm just not sure.

There are times when I fear that Siobhan and her friends simply do not have the intellectual challenges and rigour that previous ages had: that discipline of early and long-term study of a second or third language, that reliance on reading long-form books rather than short-form screens, those teachers who pushed and challenged them, those rote tasks and the attendant training that led people toward preserving moments in their memory – the memory that allows us to learn, grow and have historical context.

MEMORY, IN ROMAN GARB

Memory by Olin Levi Warner (1844-96), a bronze door at the main entrance of the Library of Congress, Washington DC.

Latin is the "language of the intellect," says Nicholas Ostler. "Latin trains the brain," says Simon James. "Latin offers grand, imaginative poetry on noble themes and marvelous myths and fierce battles," says Elaine Fantham. Does Siobhan have such inspiration now, such opportunity to exercise the brain? Are we parents – am I – too soft on our kids, too indulgent with them, too unwilling to demand more out of them?

Despite this ominous sense that I sometimes have, there are just as many times that I sit in awe of the multitude of wisdoms and talents and insights that I see every day in Siobhan and her friends. She and her friends seem completely comfortable juggling conflicting interests and tasks: school, extracurricular activities, familial responsibilities, their own changing bodies and shape-shifting friendships, et cetera. They seem unperturbed by having to navigate through the various choices, obstacles and provocations we parents throw at them. And Siobhan and all of her friends seem to be doing really well in school. Anything less than a mark in the high 80s, and Siobhan is quite disappointed.

When the great Roman historian Livy sat down to write what was to become his 142-volume history of Rome, he surely gave thought to the extensive reach and lofty ambitions of his enterprise, and to his responsibility as a memoirist for the greatest empire the world had ever known. He also felt deeply about what he was writing. As he says at the beginning of Book Thirty-One, having just taken leave of writing about the Punic War, "I somehow feel I have personally taken part in its hardships and dangers!"

In contrast, Siobhan, like many teenagers, look today to the tweets of celebrities, and the gossip that is everywhere present on TV and the Internet, for entertainment but sometimes also for knowledge and inspiration. Should she really care what Rihanna tweets about love, or what Ashton Kutcher's handlers tweet about his fame, or what the rapper Ludacris tweets about his new album? The fact is that it doesn't really matter what parents think or worry about when it comes to many of their kids' online habits. Kids follow their own instincts and interests, as they always have. Helping foster the overarching work ethic of Livy in our children is asking too much. But sometimes parents can influence their children's pathways a bit.

LIVY LIVES ON

Livy was born in 64 or 59 BCE and died in 17 CE. Most of those years went into composing his 142-volume history of the city of Rome, although only 35 books survive in their entirety. Livy became so famous in his time that, according to Pliny the Younger, a man once travelled from Cadiz, Spain, to Rome just to look at him. Once he had seen Livy, the man apparently turned around and went back home.

When Siobhan was about four or five years old and we were driving around in the car – to or from her ballet class, off to visit my sister (her godmother) in Guelph, or scooting between errands – we used to play tic-tac-toe from memory, without pen or paper. One of us would start:

"I put my 'X' in the bottom right corner."

"Okay, then I put my 'O' in the middle top."

"My 'X' goes in the bottom left."

And so on, until either she or I or the "cat" won.

It's a quick, simple game to work on the memory because of course you are simultaneously training your temporal and your spatial memory. The game is short enough to keep you interested, is not as difficult as it may first seem, and I was always happy to know that both she and I were pushing our brains around and keeping them moving. Of course we also played other driving games, as most families do – singing songs, counting the number of yellow cars we saw, working our way through the alphabet one word at a time ("A" is for alligator, "B" is for broccoli, "C" is for California, always starting from the beginning of the alphabet each time) – but the tic-tac-toe games I always found the most fun. And we always kept track of how many games each of us had won. That was the easiest thing to remember. And as any parent knows, there is great joy in having your young child say to you: "I won!" or "I beat you!"

The one foreign language, the large swath of knowledge that Siobhan knows and that I will never know, is music. Playing an instrument requires a prodigious amount of physical, intellectual and emotional memory. Since she was a very young girl, just barely able to walk, Siobhan has been interested in the piano, and there are photos of her sitting in the lap of her maternal grandfather at the family stand-up Heintzman piano. He could play rousing renditions of Newfoundland folk songs and a lively assortment of other tunes. These songs, their vibrations, their liveliness, the simple black and white verticals in front of her that became the keys to new worlds of sound and rhythm and movement, entered into her brain before she could even speak. Her early listening, her early plunking away randomly at the piano, led her, I think, to have some later facility navigating the complexities of scales and chords and the intricate play of complementary and contrasting sounds.

Siobhan started taking formal piano lessons when she was about five. She finished Grade 9 piano through the Royal Conservatory of Music program, playing her way through a vast repertoire, including works by Johann Sebastian Bach, Franz Schubert and Claude Debussy, and many other classical and contemporary artists.

I have never had any musical ability. I mean none. I remember with some pain the few weeks I tried to play the recorder in Grade 5, and even more pain when I recall the director of our high school musical looking directly at me (even though I had a speaking part in *West Side Story*, I was still expected to be a member of the chorus) and saying: "You, in the back row, just mouth the words. Please don't sing." I do not think I could find middle "C" on a piano if you paid me. In fact, I am sure that I could not.

And yet when I listen to Siobhan practicing in the next room, or I look over her shoulder

WHEN MEMORY GETS STUCK IN THE STICKS

In my mid-50s, how is it possible not to get stuck among the undergrowth and the conjugations of "new" languages? Here are three that all look like "Greek to me" (as Casca says in Shakespeare's play *Julius Caesar*).

From the Aleppo Codex – a 10th-century Hebrew Bible (Joshua 1:1).

The beginning of J. S. Bach's Violin Sonata No. 1 in G minor, in his own hand.

```
-<cp:corePropertiesxmlns:cp="http://schemas.openxmlformats.org/
package/2011/metadata/core-properties"xmlns:dc=
"http://purl.org/dc/elements/1.1/"xmlns:dcterms=
"http://purl.org/dc/terms/"xmlns:dcmitype="http://purl.org/dc/
//www.w3.org/2009/XMLSchema-instance">
  <cp:lastModifiedBy>User</cp:lastModifiedBy>
  <cp:revision>2</cp:revision>
```

Some computer code written for a virtual world.

when she is at the piano, I am amazed that she can take these curious marks on paper – treble clefs, half-notes, and whatever else they're called – and turn them into marvelous and enveloping music.

"See, Dad, it's not that complicated. Here is the part for the right hand, and here is the part for the left hand. This mark here tells you how quick the tempo should be, this mark tells you how long you hold the note, this mark tells you ..." and I am quickly at sea, with these strange words and ideas washing over me, leaving me disoriented and just a tad seasick.

"Yes," I lie to her. "I think I know what you mean. Umm … let's work on all those musical terms later. For now, can you play that song that you're learning? What's the name of it again?"

"Oh, do you mean the Chopin étude or the music from *The Piano* by Michael Nyman?"

"Either one, Sweets. I'll take either one."

Although my childhood exposure to learning a musical instrument was all but non-existent, I am pleased that Siobhan had this experience and the long-term benefits that came with it. According to leading experts in neuro-education, children aged 4-6 showed significant improvement in "verbal intelligence," as well as increased accuracy and reaction time, after only 20 days of music-based training. The study, "Short-Term Music Training Enhances Verbal Intelligence and Executive Function," was recently published in *Psychological Science*. The researchers noted that "music training requires high levels of control, attention, and memorization" and that the benefits of this training may be lifelong, since "there is a strong relationship between IQ evaluated at age 5 … and IQ evaluated later in life." Most parents want to see their children achieve more than they did. As for learning music and wandering among its past and current relics, Siobhan is exploring worlds that I will never fully be able to appreciate.

Of course not every child has access to music lessons and the support of their parents in such pursuits. Despite that, many kids choose to learn vast swaths of information because it suits them or because they find the material interesting. I've known kids aged four who could rattle off the names and characteristics of 20 different dinosaurs, and kids aged seven who could recite detailed statistics related to their favourite hockey or baseball player, and kids aged 10 who have what seems to me to be encyclo-pedic knowledge of computer programming or the intricacies of various massively multiplayer online role-playing games such as "World of Warcraft."

That game has well over 10 million subscribers and many of them have levels of knowledge about the game that would make most parents' heads swirl. If you do want to know how to navigate the intricacies of the Mists of Pandaria – the Wandering Isle, the Jade Forest, the Valley of the Four Winds or Kun-Lai Summit – or if you need to know more about the Corrupted Blood Plague incident, the Zul'Gurub dungeon or the god Hakkar the Soulflayer, you'll have to ask your kid. I'm not sure it takes any less intelligence or instinct to learn these intricacies than it does to follow Ovid's *Metamorphoses*, as it wanders through tales of goat-footed Pan, a certain Procrustian bed, the Myrmidons (a race of men created by Jove from ants), three-headed Cerberus, the snaky Medusa, the rapacious Scylla and the ship-devouring Charybdis.

The other thing that we forget, or choose to disregard, is that not everyone from earlier ages had such marvelous memories. Not everyone wandered around reciting Homer or Virgil. Describing one particularly long-winded aristocrat and senator by the name of Marcus Regulus, let-ter-writer Pliny the Younger talks about how Marcus had to write out his speeches because "he could not memorize them." And Pliny goes on to refer to his ancestors as "dim and unconscionably slow," surely not a sign of his respect for either their intelligence or their memories.

Seneca as well refers in one of his letters to a wealthy man, Calvisius Sabinus, who had a desperate desire to seem educated among his peers. It seems Calvisius would buy educated slaves who would supply him with quotations, because when he tried to quote something learned, "he often dried up in the middle of a phrase." According to Seneca, this gentleman had a "memory so bad that he would forget the name sometimes of Ulysses," and that he could not even keep straight whether he was talking about the Trojans or the Acheans. That's a bit like an American not remembering who George Washington was, or a Chinese national forgetting whether his ancestors were Chinese or Japanese.

Robert Graves, in his marvellous historical novel *I, Claudius*, makes reference to how the memories of the priests who were to interpret imminent portents or disasters that seemed always to be threatening Rome "seem in many instances to have been extremely faulty." So not everyone from the past had capacious and faultless memories. And that is a good thing to remember.

As for the fear that most parents have that the Internet is just filling us and our kids up with gossip and rumour, let's remember that the Internet did not invent these prurient interests – the Romans loved such stuff just as much as we do.

Tacitus is arguably one of the greatest historians who ever lived. Edward Gibbon, himself no slouching historian, called one of Tacitus' most important books, *The Histories*, an "immortal work, every sentence of which is pregnant with the deepest observations and the most lively images." And yet the translator of *The Histories* says that in it "Tacitus portrays a world governed by rumour, a world where whispered information, whether true or false, is one of the prime agents that can transform history." Rebellions, atrocities, conspiracies, feuds between senators and between generals, murder on a small scale and massacres on a large scale – all these and many more travesties are fed by the rumours, jealousies and repeated gossip that Tacitus documents.

He writes, for example, of the rumours that turned to panic in the streets of Rome under the Emperor Otho:

> Everywhere suspicion was rife, and terror invaded even the privacy of the home. But far greater was the alarm displayed in public spaces. With every fresh piece of news that rumour brought, men's feeling and the expressions on their faces changed. … when the Senate was summoned to the House, they found it extraordinarily hard always to strike the right note. … plain speaking would arouse suspicion; yet flattery would be detected by Otho.

All this while Otho was organizing the cavalry, the infantry, warships, magistrates and consuls for war with the future emperor Vitellius. This was not, to be sure, the most stable moment of the Roman Empire – Otho served as emperor for three months and Vitellius for eight months. But this passage – and its talk of rumours, suspicion and flattery – is not untypical for Tacitus.

And we should not forget the rumours, scandal and gossip that swirled around Cleopatra and her younger brothers (one of whom she married and later likely had killed); and Cleopatra and Julius Caesar (so desperate was she, then 21 years old, to meet Caesar, then 52, that she snuck into his palace rolled up inside a rug; nine months later, she gave birth to a child, Caesarion – Latin for "little Caesar"); and Cleopatra and Mark Antony (plenty of scandal and intrigue here related to their twin boys, to the control she was said to have over Antony, and to the political and military control of both Rome and Egypt).

HISTORICAL SILLINESS

We're not the only ones who revel in infantile humour, often based on bodily functions. A couple of playful Roman statues.

Relative to the Roman era, the rumours and gossip that seem omnipresent in our day really do not have much of an influence. How much really changes as a result of the Kardashians' fleeting romances, of how many times Brad and Angelina break up or get back together, of Justin Bieber's hair or purported love child? Yet in Roman times rumours and gossip could help to bring down dynasties and lead to wars and change the political allegiances of tribes and states.

Of course Siobhan sometimes revels in infantile jokes and lame TV shows and silly repetitive computer games. What kid, what adult, does not? But she and I also talk about music therapy (which she has an interest in) and specific battles from World War I (which she recently wrote a school

CLASSICAL TWEETS

Catullus, Horace, Juvenal, Martial, Seneca and other Latin authors often wrote using brief aphorisms, what I might call "classical tweets." Here a few (all 140 characters or less):

"I hate and love. You wonder, perhaps, why I'd do that? I have no idea. I just feel it."
— Catullus

"What wonders drink can perform! It unseals the heart, Tells hopes to turn into facts, makes cowards fight, Takes weight off worried minds."
— Horace

"What can I do in Rome?
I never learnt how to lie."
— Juvenal

"If you're poor now, my friend, then you'll stay poor. These days only the rich get given more."
— Martial

"Good sense is not borrowed or bought; indeed, I think that if it were for sale it would not find a buyer; but bad sense is bought every day."
— Seneca

assignment on) and items on the news related to violence against women, and a host of other topics that are far from insignificant. And as I see the expansive and inquisitive interests of her friends, she is not unique in her desire for knowledge of the wider world and the world of ideas.

I recently attended the Bat Mitzvah of a daughter of some good friends in Ottawa. Everything about the service, and the foundational knowledge of Hebrew that was required to really understand what was going on around me, was foreign to me. The large amounts of Hebrew spoken and sung (it was a Reconstructionist service), the reading of the prayer book from back to front, the informality of the service (people coming and going, laughing sometimes, talking among themselves), the use of the *tallit* (prayer shawl), and perhaps most of all the length of the service (it went on for about three hours): all these elements were curious and strange to me. Even the date of the service had mysteries. The date was simultaneously listed as October 15, 2011 and 17 Tishrei 5772. Now there is some intermingling of the past, present and future!

What I was particularly intrigued by was that the pivot point of the service, the moment around which all else revolves, was the reading of an ancient language that has been around for over 3,000 years, being read by Michal, a 13-year-old girl. The main task that she had to master was the reading and the understanding of a chunk of text that has been passed down, remembered, from generation to generation. Language acquisition, basic literacy, knowledge of words that are not used in her daily life – all this was expected to be absorbed and processed by a 13-year-old girl.

There seemed to me to be an individual and a collective act of memory going on: "שמע שמע שמע / shema, shema, shema," Jews recite. "Listen, listen, listen." As the Torah was read and as the Mourner's Kaddish was recited and as the shouts of "Mazel Tov!" reverberated across the room and across the millennia, I listened to this ancient language being recrafted and reborn in our age – an age which seems, if you don't listen carefully enough, to be only about the present.

The fact is, like Michal at her Bat Mitzvah, we all like to remember. It comes naturally to us, sometimes whether we wish it or not. Siobhan is constantly telling me about things that she remembers, from earlier that day at school, from her trip to Ireland last summer with her mother and grandmother, from the time five years ago when we went for a walk to the local High Park Zoo, somehow got locked in when the zoo was closed for the evening, and how we had to climb and then hop over the fence in what seemed to her at the time like an act of adventure and danger.

Later, I asked Rabbi Arthur Bielfeld of Toronto whether Latin had been of influence in his life. An advocate for various social justice issues, a founder of The Leo Baeck Day School, Bielfeld was invited by Dr. Martin Luther King Jr. in 1965 to lead a procession in an attempt to desegregate Marquette Park in Chicago. "I was fascinated by Latin and the windows it opened onto English grammar and Roman civilization," he says of his time studying the language at Worcester Academy, Massachusetts, in the early 1950s. "My best memories involve studying with Mr. Earle Peckham, a teacher of extraordinary exactitude, imposing bulk and personal warmth … I still have the prize book by F. R. Cowell on *Cicero and the Roman Republic* that he gave to me in a ceremony in the Warner Memorial Theatre." I asked Bielfeld if Latin had been of any assistance in his study of Hebrew. "I can't trace any direct connection to my study of Hebrew grammar," he said, "but the logic of Latin and its case endings certainly must have helped in my early absorption of Weingreen's *Practical Grammar for Classical Hebrew,* the standard text for newly arrived rabbinic students."

We remember, even if individual rulers or regimes throughout history have attempted to expunge the memory of their enemies or sometimes even a whole people. In *The Deified Claudius,* Suetonius writes about how, just after having secured power, the new emperor Claudius wanted his few days of indecision and insecurity before taking on the purple robes of power to be forgotten. Claudius "decreed therefore that everything which had been said and done during that time would be forgiven and forgotten in perpetuity." Claudius may have executed the tribunes and centurions that he feared would retell the stories he wanted forgotten, but Suetonius was still able to capture and preserve the shards of the story which yet survived.

Stephen Greenblatt, who I will reference later, has coined the phrase the "Great Vanishing" to talk about the many ways our collective written history has been obliterated, including by rains, flames and worms, as well as by ideology, ignorance and spilled wine.

The Roman senate itself, through *damnatio memoriae,* or condemnation of memory, sometimes officially attempted to erase from history all mention of elites and a few emperors that had been thought to dishonour the Roman state. Among those who received this sanction were the emperor Domitian, and the co-emperor Geta. The senate wanted to condemn the memory of both Caligula and Nero, but both condemnations were not supported by the succeeding emperors.

Although there have been some successes at expunging individual and collective memories throughout history, it doesn't always work out that the memory truly and completely disappears. In our own age, it has become almost impossible to erase the memory of an individual, although the attempts continue. The names Hosni Mubarak and his wife Suzanne were erased from all Egyptian monuments after they were deposed in 2011, and the image of Jerry Sandusky, a football coach at Penn State University who was accused of child rape, was recently painted over on a mural at the university, and all the wins of the head coach, Joe Paterno (for many years the paragon of winning with honour) have been retroactively cancelled. And Lance Armstrong's victories in the Tour de France have all been stripped from the record book.

MEMORY OF THE WORLD

Launched in 1992, UNESCO's Memory of the World Programme preserves and protects the world's documentary heritage. Among the items in its register:

The *Tabula Peutingeriana*, a map showing the road network of the Roman Empire. The original map was thought to be the product of Marcus Agrippa, a friend of Augustus. The version that exists dates from the fifth century. This detail shows parts of the Dalmatian coast, the Adriatic Sea, southern Italy, Sicily, and the northern African coast.

The *Universalis Cosmographia*, a world map of 1507, the first to depict a Western Hemisphere. This new world was named "America" after the great Italian explorer Amerigo Vespucci.

The Bayeux Tapestry, which depicts events leading up to the Norman Conquest of England. Commissioned in the 1070s, the cloth measures about 230 feet long. This detail, ISTI MIRANT STELLA ("People looking in wonder at the star") depicts the first recorded sighting of what we now know as Halley's Comet.

"**R**ead it again. Read it again." Every parent who has ever read to a young child knows this enthusiastic request, from an imagination in the process of forming itself. It's the voice of the child who wants to hear, yet again, the reading of a book that you have already read to them innumerable times before.

We may remember different things than what our parents want us to, or we may remember things that cause us endless labyrinths of sorrow or angst, or we may remember fleeting moments of inconsequential triumph (for me, the smallest member of my Grade 8 football team, stuck in the game for a few plays as a defensive halfback, it was and remains the "glory" of catching an interception during one of our three games that season), but we do remember.

Cynthia Good, the former publisher of Penguin Books Canada and an interviewee for this book, put it very succinctly when I asked her about whether she enjoyed studying Latin as a high school student. "I liked memorizing things," she said. When I asked about her favourite Latin phrase from her student days, her response was instantaneous: "*'Quid rides? Mutato nomine, de tefebula narrator'*, which means 'Why do you laugh? With the name changed, the story is about you.'" And then later in the interview, in the midst of one of my more academic questions, she started, unbidden, to sing:

> *Rudolphus rubrinasus fulgentissi monaso,*
> *vidisti et si eum dicas quoque candere …*

The Latin version of "Rudolph the Red-Nosed Reindeer" bubbled up from her memory, as fresh, it seemed, as when she had first learned and sung it in high school.

In a recent issue of *Wired*, Internet commentator Jonah Lehrer discussed research by Professor Betsy Sparrow and her team at Columbia University on how the Internet and Google are "ruining" (perhaps) our memory. If Google remembers everything for us, goes the logic, why should we spend valuable space in our own minds remembering? As Lehrer states, "The scientists demonstrated that the availability of the Internet is changing the nature of what we remember, making us more likely to recall *where* the facts are rather than the facts themselves." The Internet is having, in a sense, a sort of "amnesiac" effect on us.

Acknowledging our finite memory capabilities and how we are always looking for ways not to remember stuff, perhaps Google is not "rotting" our brains, but in fact creating room for other cerebral activities. As Lehrer states: "I think it shows that we're wise enough to outsource a skill we're not very good at." One of the commentators on the *Wired* website captured the ideal end result quite succinctly: The less trivia and mundane facts that one has to remember, the more the brain is freed up to store and work on "ideas." Of course all of this commentary has itself come into question, as Lehrer was recently caught in a serious, career-limiting case of plagiarism – itself a pretty elemental form

NOT ALL TWEETS HAVE LASTING VALUE

"...we came across the word 'twitter,' and it was just perfect. The definition was 'a short burst of inconsequential information,' and 'chirps from birds.' And that's exactly what the product was."
– Jack Dorsey, creator of Twitter

A Texas research firm recently analyzed 2,000 U.S. tweets over a two-week period. They separated the tweets into six categories:

- Pointless Babble – 40%
- Conversational – 38%
- Pass-along value – 9%
- Self-promotion – 6%
- Spam – 4%
- News – 4%

Although most tweets are, to put it nicely, ephemeral, we should also realize that very few people ever had time for all of Livy's 142 books. Even in Livy's own time, people were already consulting synopses of the books, in preference to the whole work. The Roman poet Martial states that he has no room on his bookcase for all of Livy, and instead prefers an abbreviated copy, in "one small volume."

of forgetting – which has led some people to go back through all his previously published writing to seek out transgressions of one sort or another.

Even now, although we don't play tic-tac-toe anymore, Siobhan and I play silly memory games based on mundane facts (about as far away from "ideas" as we can get). We'll see a licence plate and then challenge ourselves to remember it: five minutes from the moment we first saw it, and then later that day, and the following day, and a couple of weeks later.

"Dad, do you remember the licence plate?" she'll ask me over dinner. Or I'll add a "P.S." at the bottom of a note I've left her about what time I'm coming home that day: "Scoops, what is the licence plate? Write it here: _____." Sometimes we both remember that we haven't asked each other about the licence plate for a while. "Hey, what about the licence plate?" one of us will ask. "OK, let's say it both together." And we do.

I believe that the specific can invoke the universal, and that the universal can invoke the specific. I hope that when Siobhan gets older she remembers these trivial, fleeting memory games that we used to play – and perhaps realizes that there are big ideas woven into the desire of a father and his daughter trying to remember a licence plate, or the miniscule mental gymnastics necessary to play tic-tac-toe without the use of paper or pencil.

What I enjoy thinking about is how, at the age of 14, Siobhan is creating memories that will stay with her as she gets older. Siobhan is the centre of her world, the centre of the world. As she learns Latin, she augments her world, and she augments the world. She embroiders this world of hers with her own thread and her own colours. She simultaneously is part of the remembering of the lost world of Latin and the creator of her new world of memories.

The amount of information, facts, stories and ideas that have been lost is, of course, incalculable. But is that such a bad thing? Isn't it every generation's job, every family's job, every individual's job, to create and populate the world?

By the way, when I sent an email to Jonah Lehrer, who I had always considered one of the most thoughtful of Internet commentators, asking him if he had ever studied Latin (surely, I thought, such a bright guy as this – a Rhodes Scholar, the author of *Proust Was a Neuroscientist* – must have studied Latin) he responded: "Sadly, I did not."

VOCABULARY LESSON

game – n. ludus
history – n. historia
language – n. lingua
memory – n. memoria
music – n. musica

PRACTICING THE LANGUAGE

People like to read, remember and recount history.
Placet nobis res gestas antiquorum legere, repetere et enarrare.

Perhaps I should not worry so much that we, collectively and individually, are allowing our brains to seemingly flounder, are allowing slippage to occur – from the amount of memory necessary to appreciate Livy's 142 books to that necessary for appreciating only the meagreness of the latest 140-character tweet. The world's memory, and the memory of the individuals within it (including, I suppose, even Siobhan and me), is constantly in flux, is constantly being built and destroyed. Before there was a person (or persons) named Homer, there were people creating, reciting, forgetting and improvising *The Iliad* and *The Odyssey*, the oldest works of Western literature.

At the basis of George Santayana's famous statement "Those who cannot remember the past are condemned to repeat it" is the understanding that we do, often, not remember the past, that we are often incapable of remembering the lessons and implications of the past, and that we are constantly creating our world from the misremembered fragments of the past.

One of the joys of the twitterverse is historians and others who tweet past moments of history, sometimes at exactly the moment they happened (50 or 100 or 200 years previously). There have been blow-by-blow tweets of the American Civil War, of Robert Falcon Scott's doomed 1911 expedition to the South Pole, of Hitler's madness during World War II, of the eruption of Vesuvius as told by Pliny the Elder, as well as tweets from Samuel Pepys, John Quincy Adams, Winston Churchill, and even god (God?). In our day, perhaps our understanding of history and memory is appropriately summed up by the tag-line of TwHistory, an educational website which reenacted the Battle of Gettysburg and other historical events, in salvoes of up to 140 characters: "Those who forget history are doomed to retweet it."

CHAPTER FOUR

DEFECTIVE AND IRREGULAR:
SOME TENSE STUDYING

"He did not, indeed, keep silent on the subject of his own stupidity."
Suetonius, *The Deified Claudius*

"Life is really a bitch."
Catullus, "38"

S TUDYING IS HARD. The discipline, concentration and self-moti-
vation required by high school courses are not for most parents. I
certainly think that they are way too much for me.

Here I am taking precisely one course – not navigating through the
multitude of other pressures that students do, including juggling multiple
other class assignments, keeping a few extra-curricular activities going,
coping with a changing body, fending off peer pressures from friends who
may be drinking or doing drugs, and engulfed by thoughts about sex and
… well, more sex – and I am barely keeping up. In fact, many days I simply
do not keep up with the rather simple vocab work I need to do, or with the
"Practicing the Language" assignments that the *CLC* asks me to do.

Here, for example, is the practice session from Chapter One of my high school textbook:

Clemens … laborat.	in via
Caecilius … scribit.	in horto
Canis … latrat.	in atrio
Metella … stat.	in tablino
Coquus est …	in culina
Quintus est …	in triclinio

We are asked to supply the suitable word or phrase from the right-hand side to complete the sentence, and then translate the sentence. The correct answers are as follows (I know they are correct because Siobhan helped me with them):

Clemens in horto laborat. (Clemens is working in the garden.)
Caecilius in tablino scribit. (Caecilius is writing in the study.)
Canis in via latrat. (The dog is barking in the street.)
Metella in atrio stat. (Metella is standing in the atrium.)
Coquus est in culina. (The cook is in the kitchen.)
Quintus est in triclinio. (Quintus is in the bedroom.)

I'm seeing Latin everywhere in my daily life and yet I am having trouble doing the most elementary exercises from Chapter One! Of course I know all the old clichés about how "practice makes perfect," and "education is a life-long process." But even at this early stage of studying Latin I am most conscious of that other chestnut: "education is the process of discovering how much we don't know." Most days I really am wondering why I chose to accompany Siobhan on this infernal linguistic odyssey.

POMPEII ENTERTAINMENTS

Some playful words, games and drawings from the walls of Pompeii.

Siobhan has taken quite effortlessly to correcting my pronunciation, whenever I do attempt to study with her. I pronounce the head of the Pompeii household "Caecilius" with both of the "C" sounds soft. "Umm, Dad, it's pronounced 'Kaekilius', as though the 'C' sounds are both hard. Usually the 'C' sound is hard."

"Okay, thanks."

"Well, you're not in the class so I'm not surprised you don't know that. And don't forget that 'V' is pronounced like a 'W' – so the word for slave, 'servus' is pronounced like it's spelled 'serwus'."

"Okay, I'll try and remember that. So that means that Caesar's famous line, 'I came, I saw, I conquered' should really be pronounced 'weni widi wici'?"

"Yep, that's right."

"Wow. Never knew that."

As a way to keep my studying on track and focused, I try to figure out a few games or exercises that may help. In his sparkling book *Daily Life in Ancient Rome* (one of the main inspirations for *A Funny Thing Happened on the Way to the Forum*), Jerome Carcopino says that one tutor, in an attempt to make learning easier for his pupil, devised a procession of the household slaves "each of whom carried on his back an immense placard bearing in giant size one of the twenty-four letters of the Latin alphabet." Perhaps I could use that technique to help me with my vocab, or maybe I could have my own collection of slaves each display a word that I could rearrange at will to help me learn the most elegant Latin word order.

The great Roman rhetorician Quintilian, acknowledging the challenges of learning the language, came up with a great way to help little kids learn. He suggested alphabets of ivory or of pastry to help students learn!

WWW

According to *1066 and All That*, the spoof of British history written by W. C. Sellar and R. J. Yeatman, Julius Caesar found the Britons "weeny, weedy and weaky."

STUDYING LATIN CAN BE A PAIN IN THE TASK...

"I set myself to study Latin – a painful task."

Apuleius, *The Golden Ass*

...BUT LEARNING ENGLISH IS NO WALK IN THE PARK

When one is "of a certain age," studying Latin, or any new language, is difficult. But it's also wise to remember how hard English would be to learn.

George Bernard Shaw once observed that the word "fish" could be spelled "ghoti" by using the "gh" from the word "enough," the "o" from "women," and the "ti" from "nation."

The early writings and cartoons of Dr. Seuss have been gathered into a book called *The Tough Coughs as He Ploughs the Dough*. Acknowledging the many pronunciations of "ou" and "gh," the book's title is meant to be pronounced: *The Tuff Cuffs as He Pluffs the Duff.*

Sounds delicious to me. And perhaps linguistically beneficial.

Young girls are constantly playing elaborate rhyming and clapping games. I was always impressed with the intricate games that Siobhan used to play when she was about 5 or 6, sometimes with one girl, sometimes with two or three. One of my favourites was "Down By the Bay":

> Down by the bay,
> Where the watermelons grow,
> Back to my home,
> I dare not go.
> Because if I do,
> My mother will say,
> "Did you ever see a bear combing his hair?"

With the hair-combing bear line replaced with other silly lines:

"Did you ever see a goose kissing a moose?"
"Did you ever see a whale with a polka dot tail?"
"Did you ever see a pig wearing a wig?"
"Did you ever see a cat wearing a hat?"

"Did you ever see a dragon pulling a wagon?"
And so on, with the song sometimes ending with:
"Did you ever have a time when you couldn't find a rhyme?"

And another clapping game that she and her friends used to sing, enjoying the hints at "bad words" almost sneaking into the song:

Miss Suzie had a steamboat
The steamboat had a bell
Miss Suzie went to heaven
The steamboat went to
Hello operator
Please give me number nine
If you disconnect me
I'll kick you from
Behind the Iron Curtain there was a piece of glass
When Suzie sat upon it she cut her little
Ask me no more questions
Tell me no more lies
The boys are in the bathroom zipping up their
Flies are in the meadow
The bees are in the park
Miss Suzie and her boyfriend are kissing in the
Dark is like a movie
A movie's like a show
A show is like a TV screen
And that is all I know!

Only now am I beginning to appreciate the purpose behind those rhythmic songs, rhyming words and intricate claps – it's a very simple and fun way to learn new words and figure out how they fit together. The newly formed pathways of the memory, discussed in greater length in the previous chapter, are also of course called into service in these joyful, sing-song games. And as the great literary critic Northrop Frye reminds us, more fundamental patterns are also at work. In his six radio talks collected in the book *The Educated Imagination*, Frye talks about how poetry – not prose and not the applied language of ordinary life – is at the "centre" of literature:

> Poetry is the most direct and simple means of expressing oneself in words. ... prose is a much less natural way of speaking than poetry is. If you listen to small children, and to the amount of chanting and singsong in their speech, you'll see what I mean.

I have not come up with any such lively or delightful songs that have helped me study Latin, or that have helped me absorb the rhythms of the language. I was interested however to read that Roman soldiers sang songs to help them with their marching, sometimes to the rhythm we associate with the tune "Oh My Darling Clementine." In Suetonius's *Lives of the Caesars* we learn that Julius Caesar's soldiers sang songs as they marched, sometimes combining stories of military conquest with subtle and not-so-subtle references to Caesar's sexual conquests. There was some sexual intrigue, for example, related to Caesar's stay with King Nicomedes, and after their conquest of Gaul, Caesar's soldiers sang the following as they marched behind his chariot:

> Caesar had his way with Gaul;
> Nicomedes had his way with Caesar;
> Behold now Caesar, conqueror of Gaul, in triumph,
> Not so, Nicomedes, conqueror of Caesar.

As for Caesar's reputation with the ladies (including, of course, Cleopatra, but also with other queens, wives of his friends and rivals, and a vast swath of commoners throughout the Roman provinces), the soldiers returning from another military conquest used to sing the following little marching ditty to help keep them in step:

> Men of Rome, look out for your wives;
> We're bringing the bald adulterer home.

In Gaul you fucked your way through a fortune,
Which you borrowed here in Rome.

One of my interviewees for this book, Carlos, studied Latin in Buenos Aires and he had his own inspiration for studying the language. "My teacher," he told me "was absolutely beautiful. I used to sit at the front of the class, right in front of her. Oh, I enjoyed when she crossed her legs!" Carlos, now a psychiatrist specializing in the diagnosis, treatment, and rehabilitation of the mind and mental illness, had to take Latin. "I took one year of Latin and one year of Greek – it was compulsory." His memories of studying the language, and that delightful crossing and uncrossing of those legs, led me to think that perhaps there are various ways to inspire and excite people as they study.

Dr. Ruth, the effervescent international authority on sex, also had some insights on the language she uses to disseminate information about her area of expertise. Growing up during World War II, she never had the opportunity to study Latin, but she uses Latin words in her many books about sex and sexual literacy. As she told me:

ROMANCING THE LANGUAGE

Because of the varying ways to classify languages and dialects, it is impossible to come up with a firm number of Romance languages (that is, languages that are derived from Latin), but here is an overview of some major ones, and the number of current speakers:

Spanish (330 million)
Portuguese (180 million)
French (70 million)
Italian (65 million)
Rumanian (25 million)
Catalan (12 million)

It is estimated that there are about 800 million native speakers of Romance languages worldwide, speaking about 50 different Romance languages. Many more Romance languages existed previously, but have now become extinct.

Even though up to 60 percent of English words come to us from or through Latin, English is not a Romance language; it's a Germanic language.

I was born in 1928 in Germany in those terrible years before the war and the Holocaust. When I was ten, my father was taken by the Nazis, and my mother then sent me to Switzerland, where I spent my high school years in an orphanage. So I never even finished high school and had no opportunity to study Latin. But education has always been important to me and I encouraged my daughter Miriam to study Latin. I still remember her high school Latin teacher, and talking with her about which university would be good for Miriam. Even though I never studied Latin, I've used lots of Latin words in my books. Sex education is full of them: coitus interruptus, mons pubis, and so many more! I've authored over 30 books – but none have been translated into Latin yet! Maybe I should write a new book, *Sex for Latin Lovers!*

Ruth's daughter Miriam studied Latin under Miss Nivens at Barnard School for Girls in New York City. The feeling for education was obviously passed on from mother to daughter. Miriam is now the Director of the Home Instruction Program for Preschool Youngsters, a home-based, family literacy program originally developed in Israel that currently operates in 10 countries. "A love of learning begins early and it begins at home," Miriam told me. "I believe anything our society can do to help all parents engage with their very young children around books and extensive language use is an important step towards creating a more equal society."

In the midst of all this wisdom on the things that inspire kids to learn Latin, I was still not studying the language with any commitment. Wandering around the Internet for inspiration, I discovered a great sentence that was about at my level:

Malo malo malo malo.

Now here was something I could sink my abecedarian baby teeth into! "*Malo,*" I read, is the first-person singular of the verb *malle*, for "I prefer"; it is also in the ablative, the place where, for "apple tree"; and as the ablative of comparison, it means "naughty or evil"; and it is an ablative

THE GROWTH OF LATIN

**Language Map
of Ancient Italy
c. 400 BCE**

Labels on map: Raetic, Venetic, Gualish, Ligurian, Etruscan, Umbrian, Picene, Sabine, Various smaller languages, including Aequiam, Faliscan, Hernican, Marrucinian, Paelignian and Vestinian, LATIN →, Volscian, Oscan, Messapic, Greek, Greek, Sicel, Greek

Until about the third century BCE, Latin was just one among many ancient Italic languages. It was spoken in a small spot of land around present-day Rome, and was certainly in much less use than Etruscan and Oscan, long since forgotten.

Countries that speak Romance languages now (for example, Rumanian and Spanish) and countries where one of the official languages is a Romance language (for example, Canada, where French is an official language). Other Romance languages widely used include French in current-day Cambodia, Laos and Vietnam (formerly known as "French Indochina"), and Spanish across the United States.

**Where Latin-Inspired Romance
Languages Are Now Spoken**

of condition. So that eloquent and well-crafted phrase "Malo malo malo malo" means "I'd rather be in an apple tree than a naughty boy struggling with adversity." Perhaps it wasn't a sentence that I could use too often, but one day I'll use it.

I also started to look through other high school textbooks. My brother-in-law Howard loaned me a textbook, *Selected Latin Readings*, originally published in 1953. The book was edited by two teachers at an elite local high school, the University of Toronto Schools, which still offers Latin and which I'll be referencing later in these pages. What is particularly sobering (and really of no inspiration to me at all) is that in the Acknowledgements an assortment of teachers from various high schools are thanked for their help – and most of them have long ceased to offer Latin to their students, including Bathurst Heights Collegiate Institute, Harbord Collegiate Institute, Beamsville High School and Bowmanville High School, to name just a few.

Howard also spoke of a time not too long ago when everyone, it seemed, used to know some Latin. He mentioned that he and his friends used to hang out at the local pub, The Albion, in Guelph. "Whenever we had a disagreement about a Latin word, or when we weren't sure of the proper ending of a verb, we just asked the bartender – and she'd always set us straight … she knew her Latin."

William Krehm, a 100-year-old businessman and former Trotskyite who I will discuss in greater length in the pages to come, has picked up over the years a variety of languages, including of course Latin, and I thought he might provide a speck of encouragement. He noted that the one language he was having some difficulty with was Chinese. "If I was ten years younger I would go and live in China for a year to learn the language," he said to me. So there is perhaps some hope and optimism that I need to preserve in my delinquent attempts to learn Latin. Even in my 90s I may still have this curious linguistic itch, even if it never gets scratched very efficiently or satisfyingly.

I was also captivated to learn how far and wide the language had traveled around the globe. I interviewed Johann Peisl, an Emeritus Professor of Physics at Ludwig-Maximilians-Universität, Munich. Werner Heisenberg was an honorary professor at the university when Johann first became a professor there, and Johann held the same Chair of Physics that was earlier held by Wilhelm Röntgen, discoverer of X-rays, who, in 1901, was the first winner of the Nobel Prize in Physics. Although Latin was of use to Johann as a physicist, he did not think studying it was the best use of his time, and he thought he should have spent his time studying other languages currently in use. "It was ridiculous to have spent years studying Latin, when I could have been studying other languages such as Italian and French. I told my two daughters – who both became artists – not to study Latin."

FOREIGN LANGUAGES, THEN AND NOW

Beginning of the Book of Genesis in the Gutenberg Bible (it's Latin, of course)

Text messages from www.urbandictionary. com:

LYK OMG did U C TWILIGHT YET? ITZ SO FREAKIN KILL!

OMG LYK WHY CANT I UZ SHIFT TO LYK PROPERLY CAPITALIZE MY SENTNCES?!?!?CAPS LOCK IS JUST LYK SOOOOO COOOOL THAT I MUST TYP EVRYTINK I EVR THINK OF WIT IT???!?!

"Dude LOL lmfaorOFL!!!"

Peisl did, however, love learning Latin because of his teacher. "Most of the teachers who taught Latin when I was in school were Nazis, and were not allowed to teach right after World War II," he told me. "So an already retired teacher had been reactivated to teach us Latin."

I spoke with a woman named Corina, who I met at the Staatliche Antikensammlungen, the State Museum of Antiquities, in Munich. She had studied Latin for four years as a teenager in Transylvania. She talked fondly of her fellow Rumanians Constantin Brâncusi and Eugène Ionesco, and also of her English, French, German and Rumanian language studies.

I interviewed a woman named Cookie Diestel, who studied Latin in China between the wars at the Shanghai British School. Earlier her mother had attended the same school when it was known as The Cathedral School for Girls and she too studied Latin there. Cookie's father, originally from Germany, was a "tea taster" in China. And I met a theoretical physicist who studied Latin in South Africa, and a technology consultant who studied Latin in his home country of Iceland, who I will refer to again in the coming pages.

And I went back to Siobhan. I didn't really want to attend class with her, but I did think that if I had the chance to sit in on one of her classes, maybe just once, and had the opportunity to ask some of her fellow students about their study habits, it might help me. She was not happy, and my attempt at some offhand, jovial comments about sitting in on her class did not go over well. "You're being really immature right now," she said. "You cannot, cannot, sit in on my class. Ask Mom what she thinks, because I'm sure she'll agree with me."

Unfortunately, Siobhan was right. Sheilagh was definitive on the topic: "Excuse me," she helpfully responded to my request, "but that issue is implicitly and explicitly referenced in your standing agreement. You are seriously trying to bend your privileges here. I'm with Siobhan on this."

Youth may be wasted on the young, but so too education may be wasted on the old. After a certain age, and certainly by the time one has reached one's 50s, (and despite William Krehm's idea about learning Chinese in one's 80s) perhaps learning new things, new languages, is both not easy and not to be attempted. When I am feeling particularly beat up by the language, when I realize that studying long-abandoned languages is not for everyone, I do take some comfort knowing that not everyone has always been so convinced of the benefits of Latin, including several people I've already mentioned. Although Roger Ascham, Queen Elizabeth I's tutor, said that "All men covet to have their children speak Latin," the great Irish poet and playwright W. B. Yeats, speaking to his son's schoolmaster, said: "Do not teach him one word of Latin." Yeats was convinced that Latin would only cloud his son's natural impulses to learn Gaelic, and may even do much worse. "The Roman people," said Yeats, "were the classic decadence, their literature form without matter." And he went on, talking about the "Latin miasma." Referencing Bertrand Russell, who Yeats considered a "featherhead," he thought that study of Latin would leave his son "helpless." I'm not sure how Yeats came to all his conclusions, but he certainly was adamant that Latin could do his son no good.

FLAUBERT DEFINES LATIN

"LATIN: The natural speech of man. Spoils one's style. Useful only for reading inscriptions on public buildings. Beware of quoting Latin tags: they all have something risqué in them." (from the "Dictionary of Received Ideas")

Bishop Ferdinand Fonseca of Mumbai, who studied Latin in India under British rule in the early 1940s, noted in a letter to me how he had to "study by heart the declensions and conjugations of the Latin nouns, adjectives and verbs." And he didn't hide the challenges – "It was pretty difficult," he said. Alain de Botton, the Swiss writer, documentary maker, author of *How Proust Can Change Your Life*, *Religion for Atheists* and other books, does not have good memories of the process. "I was terribly taught at Latin and loathed it for silly, superficial reasons," he said to me in an email. "I am traumatised by the whole subject and am hoping that I'll be able to do better for my own kids."

Sir Harry Kroto, who won the Nobel Prize in Chemistry in 1996 for his discovery of the spherical molecule Buckminsterfullerene, which has been so important for nanotechnology and our digital age, considers that his time studying Latin could have been better spent. He told me: "I do not think it particularly useful – compared to many, many, many other things one could study. I did not like it and found it tedious and rather boring and only did it because it was necessary at the time for entry to Oxford and Cambridge" (although he never attended either university). Kroto seemed to think that the study of Latin provided very little of value: "I am afraid I do not think it gave me any insight into anything whatsoever," he said.

When I received such dismissive comments and realized that some pretty smart people really had no time for Latin, or at least the way that they had been taught the language, I must say that I did have some joy, some relief. Perhaps I was just not made to stick my head into this hornet's nest of declensions and conjugations and arcane grammatical rules. But I can't tell Siobhan of these doubts and frustrations. At least not yet. I don't want to discourage her studies or dampen her natural enthusiasms. For the moment, maybe I'll scour the Internet and try to find a Latin translation

LOL MY BFF AND U2, S.P.Q.R.

We may sometimes think that current teenagers are the masters of abbreviations – it can save so much time when sending texts to friends: LOL, BFN, BFF, etc. But abbreviations have been with us for a few thousand years.

For the emperors and church authorities who commissioned the copying done by Roman and Medieval scribes, there was a concern to save both the raw materials (ink, writing implements) and the time spent by scribes in their task. Using abbreviations was the fastest and most efficient way for scribes to churn out the most number of words in the quickest possible time.

The 607-page *Dizionario di Abbreviature latine ed italiene* is a standard reference book for people navigating through the Latin abbreviations used. And don't think that

deciphering Latin abbreviations was as simple as just remembering that "LOL" means "Laugh Out Loud" or that "BFN" means "Bye For Now" or that BFF means "Best Friends Forever."

The letter "C" for example, could stand for any of 56 separate words: everything from Caesar (the emperor) to curia (the papal court at the Vatican in Rome).

Let's not forget that an abbreviation was even used to identify the crucified body of Jesus Christ: the letters "I.N.R.I." – which stood for "Jesus Nazarenus Rex Iudaeorum" or "Jesus Christ, King of the Jews" (in early Latin there was no distinction between the letter "I" and "J") – were placed at the top of the cross on which Jesus died.

And there were thousand of other Latin abbreviations used, including "S.P.Q.R." – Senatus Populusque Romanus (The Senate and the Roman People), which is still in use on manhole covers, and elsewhere, in the city of Rome. BFN.

for the only song I can remember singing as a kid: "One potato, two potato, three potato, four." Maybe that will engender in me at least a talent for counting in my new language. Until then, as I like to say about apple trees and adversity: "Malo malo malo malo."

VOCABULARY LESSON

difficult – adj. difficilis
discipline – n. disciplina
rule – n. praeceptum; v. rego
song – n. cantus
think – v. cogito

PRACTICING THE LANGUAGE

Why is studying this new language so difficult?
Cur mihi tam difficile est hanc linguam non mihi notam discere?

Chapter Five

A DELIGHTFUL AND NAÏVE SENSE OF THE GOOD

"I'm saying – keep playing. Live life as a song."
Plautus, *The Haunted House*

"… let her tell the story of my happiness …"
Sulpicia

THERE ARE NO TWO PEOPLE better connected, more fused, than a father and his teenaged daughter. How could there be?

They are bound by family, which at its best and most ingenious is surely the strongest connection there is. The family force is certainly stronger than gravitation, and when it is allowed to follow its own course and its own logic, it is even more powerful than the strong nuclear force, the most emphatic force in the universe.

THE GOOD

The Emperor Marcus Aurelius, from the Glyptothek, Munich.

As the strong nuclear force holds protons, neutrons and quarks together in their infinitesimal dance, so the family force holds fathers and daughters together in their own unique dance. The two distinct parts possess a fundamental, shared history: a few moments of blood, biology and excitation that they navigate together. The two parts engender and then assign to themselves a closeness – sometimes a space so slight that it is unobservable to others – that they both independently occupy and simultaneously share. An outside person seeing them walking down the street together might say: "I'm sure those two don't really speak to one another" or "That daughter and that father don't seem connected" or "There go a father and daughter on different, unconnecting paths." But these are not rigorous sightings. They are only fleeting observations from people not aware of the invariant mass, the portion of the familial iceberg hidden below the surface. They are not based on the pressures and energies that truly define objects and people in motion. And they certainly do not invoke the symmetry and coherence that determines the intricate structure of our lives.

Fathers and daughters understand each other, or are drawn by a need to understand each other: daughters know this and fathers know this. The two have enough differences to form a mutual attraction that can withstand the most difficult, the most disruptive, of actions. Because they are not trying to be like the other, and nor are they desiring to be completely unlike the other, they have their own mutually dependent orbit, their own rotational attraction. These differences mean that they are constantly moving toward one another, without actually ever coalescing. They seek and want this continuous approach, this impulse-momentum connection.

Fathers and daughters can talk about anything, or almost anything. And if the topics get too embarrassing (functions of the body, unexpressed emotions) they can be laughed off, or assigned to mothers. If the topics get too serious (death, dissolute family members) they can be delayed for a later time. If the topics get too ominous (the future, failing health) they can be woven, as appropriate, and randomly, into other conversations.

Fathers understand intimately the problems – or at least some of the big ones – that await their daughters. Every father has been a teenaged boy, and he knows, viscerally, what is swirling around in the blood and imagination of a teenaged boy. I certainly know some of these swirlings. As for girl-centred affections, I was perhaps a bit earlier than most. I first fell in "love" in Grade 4, at the age of ten, with a girl named Colleen. And when I say "love" I mean all-consuming, all-absorbing, all-enriching.

Van Morrison's song "Brown-Eyed Girl" came out in the spring of 1967 and it is forever associated in my mind with the brown-eyed Colleen who sat a few seats away from me in class. I looked at her, a lot. That's not quite on the same intellectual par as Dante composing *The Divine Comedy* in honour of Beatrice, who he first met at the age of nine, but I'll just have to accept that my artistic ambitions were more humble.

A FAMILY OF CHARACTER(S)

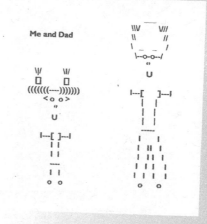

A drawing Siobhan did when she was ten years old. We've always thought these were pretty good likenesses. Later we had this image printed on a T-shirt for each of us, which we sometimes wear on Father's Day.

I fell in love again in Grade 6 with a girl named Dorothy. I fondly remember on Saturdays circling Dorothy's house on my bicycle, hoping to catch a glimpse of her. I remember imagining holding her hand, and walking next to her. I remember looking at her dark, glistening hair and trying to catch her eye and watching the way she laughed with her friends, Monica and Maureen. I said things to her (in my imagination) that I had not said to any other girl before.

And then I hit my high school years, where it seemed as though all I ever thought of was girls. I would smile dumbly at them on the bus to and from school. I would try desperately to dance with them at our high school dances. I would fall asleep thinking about being beside them and looking at them and smelling them and … well let's just say that I thought about girls a lot.

The unknown landscape sometimes enlivens the fine phrensy of the mind more than the known landscape. As a teenaged cartographer, I would have written "Here Be Angels" or "Here Be Beauty" or "Here Be Breathless Excitement and Infinite Pleasure" on the maps I would have drawn of these mysterious and undiscovered lands, these unexplored hints of unknown terra pretty firma.

So I do know, as a father, about some of the challenges and adventures and awkwardnesses that my daughter has gone through and that she will go through over her next few years. I understand them – or at least my versions of them. And Siobhan, in her own taciturn way, knows that I know about some of these things. She knows that, having some history behind me, I have an understanding of and a sympathy for the brave and strange new world through which she is currently wandering. She knows that I have always been there for her, and that I am there for her now, even if she doesn't always overtly acknowledge or depend upon the resource.

Part of this understanding means letting go. When I see Siobhan reading, or walking down the street with her friends, or hopping onto the subway heading to her piano class, I am inquisitive about her life and everything that she is thinking and doing, and simultaneously joyful at her complete independence, her separation from me and all of the ways that I might choose to sustain and increase our interactions.

Part of this sympathy means wanting to capture and preserve in some form or another the fleeting moments. One day when she was five years old and in Grade 1, Siobhan came home and started asking me about Picasso, who she and her fellow students were studying at the local school, Garden Avenue Public School. Why her Grade 1 teacher, Lindy King, was leading her young charges on a walk through the scarred landscape of "Guernica" I'll never know, although I think it had something to do with referencing Remembrance Day through one of the fiercest war paintings ever produced.

"We're studying Picasso in school, Dad," Siobhan told me. "Did you know he had a blue period, and then a rose period, but it was really more like a red period because he painted more with red? Do you have any books about him?"

When I showed her a book I had on Picasso, and when we started to look more closely at "Guernica," the conversation took on a life of its own. Siobhan pointed out the woman on the left side of the canvas, holding her child. "At first I thought that lady was holding a turtle, Dad. Now I think it's a baby. Is that her own baby she's holding? Is that baby dead? That's sad."

COVER OF SIOBHAN'S GRADE 1 PICASSO PROJECT

We also spoke about the horse at the centre of the painting – which she called a dragon – about the knife in the severed hand at the bottom, and about the various screaming faces arranged around the canvas. Siobhan showed me things about the painting that I had not seen before and I showed her things that she had not seen before.

After 15 minutes or so, we moved on to other topics, including her friends, her new pink boots, owls (which she was also studying in school), who is winning in our ongoing games of tic-tac-toe, and how she liked the newest Harry Potter movie, even though when we had gone to see it a few weeks earlier she covered her eyes and she asked me to cover her ears during the scary parts.

I was so intrigued by her ability to freely move between the frightening and the pleasant, between the good and the bad, that I wrote a small article on our conversation and sent it off to *The Toronto Star*, which published it under the title "Good, Bad and Picasso." In the article I noted how effortlessly she moved between the horror articulated by Picasso's painting and discussions we had about her ballet class, about what we were going to have for dessert and about when we were going to go kite-flying again. I thought it was important to capture some snippets of our conversations because they really do dissipate so quickly. Unless I preserved some of their substance, a few of their words, I reasoned, they really do fade to nothingness. And then I'm not sure even the Higgs boson could give them mass or so much as one quantum of energy.

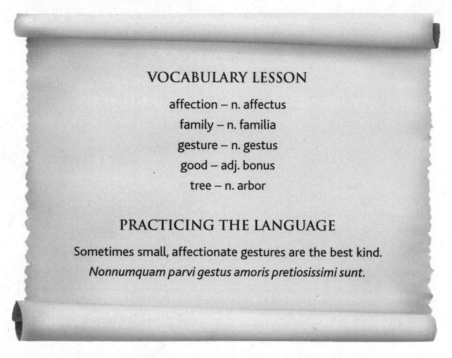

VOCABULARY LESSON

affection – n. affectus
family – n. familia
gesture – n. gestus
good – adj. bonus
tree – n. arbor

PRACTICING THE LANGUAGE

Sometimes small, affectionate gestures are the best kind.
Nonnumquam parvi gestus amoris pretiosissimi sunt.

Sometimes my attempt at preserving and capturing, or our mutual sharing, has no words attached. Or not always the words that might seem at first glance to be the most relevant. We can be talking about going for a walk or heading out for a cup of tea, when in fact what we are really talking about is our intertwined DNA and our shared history. We can be talking about making a meal together and what proportion of oil and vinegar should be used in the salad dressing, when what we are really doing is sharing the intricacies of our mutual facial features and the similar ways our imaginations graft on to one another. And sometimes words themselves are just an unnecessary encumbrance. After dinner we often head for an ice cream cone at the local video store. Summer and winter we will sit outside on the small bench that runs the length of the store – in summer there are lots of people out and we usually see someone we know. In winter, with our gloved hands wrapped around the cones and our breath clouding the air around us, there are not so many people around, so sometimes we'll just sit there in the cold, eating our cones – hers is usually Crunchy Frog (chocolate chips in mint ice cream) and mine is usually Maple Walnut (which was my mom's favourite flavour).

These days, through our mutual "studying" of Latin, I'm trying to hang on to a few of these moments. I put "studying" in quotation marks because although I am quite confident in Siobhan's study skills, and happy with her quiz and test marks so far, I am continuing to spend very little time actually studying the language. I'm reading widely (in English of course): Lucan and Lucretius, Macrobius and Martial, Terence and Tacitus. I'm talking with lots of people (sometimes I think this is my only real talent) and following leads. "Peter, I mentioned your book to a fellow I met in California and he told me you should read …" says Morden Yolles, a friend from the Cambridge Club, where I work out. "I studied Latin during high school and university," says Lance Talbot, whose father is from Nigeria, and who grew up in Sudbury. "You really should contact my old Latin teacher at Upper Canada College, Terrence Bredin – he'd love to talk with you," says David Beauroy.

So I am observing Siobhan in her expanding universe, and talking about this learning enterprise I've undertaken, but I can't say I'm doing much studying of the subject of this book. The great Transcendentalist essayist and poet Ralph Waldo Emerson, who began his formal education at the Boston Latin School, once said that language is "a city to the building of which every human being brought a stone." So far, I don't think I've brought even a pebble to the Latin language.

One Friday evening in mid-fall three of Siobhan's friends came over for dinner and a sleep-over. All of them were studying Latin so I took the opportunity to ask them a few questions about their class (after asking Siobhan her permission to do so, of course – to which she gave her somewhat grudging approval).

All the girls seemed to like the teacher, Matthew.

"Our teacher is awesome. He's fun. And he's a great storyteller in class," said Kate.

"Latin isn't dead, it's immortal!" said Alena, echoing what seemed to be a bit of in-class propaganda. "Sometimes now when I'm reading English, my Latin will help me understand words I don't know."

Catherine said she decided to take Latin because she thought it would help her writing: "I'm a creative writer and I thought Latin would help me with my writing."

Although Siobhan was moderately embarrassed by my pestering questions, her three friends didn't seem to mind too much.

Over the course of the evening, the girls spent about five hours talking. Not playing video games, not watching TV, not wanting to bake cookies or head out for a walk or phoning other friends. Just talking, and then more talking. When I asked in a faux-exasperated tone "What is it that you girls have so much to talk about!?" Alena just responded: "We're girls!" as though that explained everything. And, in a way, I guess it did.

The next morning at breakfast – Siobhan and I served our house specialty, which is crêpes, with blueberries, bananas, maple syrup, and whipped cream, all dusted with cinnamon – I continued my questioning. I asked the girls if they had any favourite Latin words.

"Venalicius" said Kate. "It means 'slave-dealer' – I like the sound of the word and the way it rolls out of the mouth."

"Circumspectat," said Alena. "It means 'to look around' and it's fun to say."

"Every time I see the letter 'V' I want to pronounce it as a 'W' – even in English words," said Catherine. "Because that's the way that letter is pronounced in Latin."

They also told me about how, in Pompeii, the brothels were very clearly marked. All shops had a picture of what they offered or sold, the girls told me. A shoemaker might have a picture of a shoe or a boot at the front of his shop, and a person selling cloth might have a picture of a shirt or a toga above the doorway. The brothels, apparently, had a picture of a penis on their front door, and the more expensive brothels had more than one penis – with the most expensive brothels having a picture of four parallel penises. And the girls also told me that as you entered the city there would be carvings made into the stones of the roadway, showing the way to the brothels. The images used? A series of penises pointing the way, of course. The Latin teacher was somehow instilling in his students both an understanding of the minutia of Latin pronunciation, and telling them stories that would keep their interest. His methods seemed to be working, at least if the enthusiasm and laughter at the breakfast table was any guide. And I guess he fully appreciates the fact that, especially when communicating with teenagers, sex sells.

After breakfast the girls talked some more, and they spent part of the time playing a rather curious form of trivia. They would toss out to each other questions about themselves:

"What is my grandmother's name?"

"Who is my favourite composer?"

"When do I get my braces off?"

It was a great way of self-celebrating and of keeping the randomness and the excitement of the conversations going. I'm not sure a group of teenaged boys would play similar games, or spend so much time just talking, but for these girls it was exactly what they wanted to do. And it was fun to overhear.

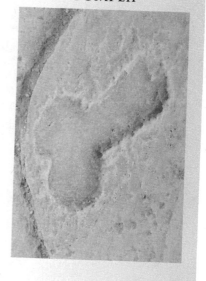

POINTING THE WAY IN POMPEII

Now that I am on this path of discovery with my daughter – or let's say that I am beginning to discover the world of Latin and that Siobhan is beginning to discover the world, of which Latin is a small part

– I'm beginning to recall various moments in the reading and writing life of my daughter. For example: that she learned how to write at about the same time that she learned how to read, and that she wrote her first words before the age of two. I remember, very clearly, talking on the phone in early December 1998, almost two years to the day after she was born, and when I put the phone down Siobhan showed me a piece of paper on which she had been writing. "Look Dad," she said. "Ho Ho Ho. This is what Santa Claus says." There on the piece of paper were indeed the words "Ho Ho Ho." The 'H's didn't look dissembled and the 'o's were closed and pretty circular. It was quite legible. I made a mental note to myself, with some pride: my daughter wrote her first words before she hit the age of two. If you ask whether this paternal pride continues to this day – well, I think you know the answer.

Of course both her mother and I read to her constantly – not such a surprise considering that we both believe strongly in education and are both active readers. A couple of years later, when Siobhan was four years old, while we were out driving around doing various errands, she started to call out words that she saw on signs that she could read. "Dad, that says 'tree'." Or "Dad, does that say 'dog'?" Or "Hey, I saw the word 'cat'!" I remember saying to her "Pretty soon, Turnip, you'll be able to read every word that you see! That will be pretty amazing when you can read every single word that you see." She wasn't sure that what I was saying was necessarily true, but I do think that she felt that her world, or the world of words, was beginning to open up and provide some wisdom and fun.

AFFECTIONATE BONDS

"Nature has formed many different attachments for us in this life ... but she has forged no bond of affection stronger than the one that binds us to our offspring."

– Macrobius, *Saturnalia*

I don't do it as much now, but when she was five or six and I was putting her to bed I used to try and remind her of something great that she did that day, or something that she might find funny or pleasing. Nothing big, just a small gesture for her to sleep on. "You are really getting great on the piano" or "wasn't that a fun story that your aunt Maureen told earlier today" or "that necklace you made is really cute – I love the way you combined the purple and the blue and the green beads" or "have a good sleep, Sweetie-Poops, and don't forget that tomorrow we are going tobogganing in the park, and then for Jell-o and hot chocolate." Just a small moment of optimism or joy that she could fold within her as she nodded off to sleep. One recent evening I was also able to recapture that small tradition by sending her off to sleep with the following: "Spoops, I am so proud of you – that you got 149 out of 149 on your big Latin vocab quiz! Have a good sleep. Love you."

One of the rituals that Siobhan has for Christmas is to give me a recording of the songs that she has learned over the previous year. The songs can be quite sophisticated and sometimes have up to 20 layers on them – with Siobhan sometimes playing multiple piano and guitar tracks, and providing all the voices and the other multiple effects that go into producing a well-crafted recording. Her use of the sound recording technology and the programs she gathers from the Internet are certainly way beyond my abilities, but she seems to handle them effortlessly. This year she also gave me a very low-tech gift. She created her own tea, from mixing various types of tea and then adding a few shakes of cinnamon. She then made four tea bags: using porous paper normally made for drip coffee, which then she sewed up by hand, using coloured thread. It must have taken her almost as much time to make the tea bags as it did to record a song. But I did find both gifts delicious and warming.

Another of the rituals that Siobhan and I have had for many years is our pizza picnics in our local park, and climbing its welcoming trees. High

Park is a grand old park, with trails that meander among the gardens and natural forests, a large pond that welcomes skaters in the winter, and a zoo that houses a small assortment of animals: American bison, emu, llamas, capybaras and mouflon sheep with their massive curling horns. In 1923, Ernest Hemingway, then a reporter on *The Toronto Star*, wrote about the park's mighty, threatened trees. "The oak is not built for compromises," he wrote. "It is like some animal of prehistoric times." He worried about the threats to the park that were coming from the growing city around it, and his article was an attempt to preserve the park's trees for future generations.

Every spring Siobhan and I climb the Japanese cherry trees, the first 2,000 of which were planted as a gift from the citizens of Tokyo to the citizens of Toronto. For a few transitory days in late April, the trees (Japanese name *sakura*; Latin name *prunus serrulata*) are bursting with pink-white and pink-purple flowers, and Siobhan and I have a few favourite, easily-climbable trees that we nudge our way up into. We take photos of the blossoms and of each other, we talk about stuff, and we remember the year before, and

IN THE TREES

From our tree-climbing expeditions, with more to come.

the year before that, when we did the same thing. We try to time our climb for those few ephemeral days when the spring winds and rains have not yet scattered the blossoms, and from a distance, or perhaps from the vantage point of a mobile "V" of Canada Geese flapping and honking overhead, the trees resemble huge, pinkish snowballs.

After we had climbed one of our favourite trees last spring, as we walked out of the park, I said to her: "Hey, Chicken-Delight, let's try and climb those trees every year. Every single year. I'm going to be 90 and you're going to be 50, but we are still going to climb those trees. I may have to bring a step-ladder and we may both have trouble getting our sorry butts up into the branches, and we may have some trouble getting down, but let's try and climb those trees every year. Too much of a crazy idea? What do you think?"

"Sounds good, Dad. Sounds like fun."

CHAPTER SIX

THE INEVITABLE (AND PREDICTABLE) BAD

"… storms of the mind toss us around daily …"
Seneca, *Letters*

"The plots are within, the danger is within, the enemy is within!"
Cicero, *In Catilinam II*

THERE IS NO RELATIONSHIP more disconnected, more confused, than that of a father and his teenaged daughter. How could there be?

The two separate entities do not share the same bodily mould, the same gendered history, and are therefore, other than a few ill-informed speculations, ignorant of how the other's mind, body and spirit work together, ignorant of what shapes the other's memories, dreams, reflections. I may imagine what it might be like to be

THE BAD

The Emperor Nero, from the Glyptothek, Munich.

91

a teenaged girl – some male filmmakers and writers have done that, and a few have done it exceedingly well – but it is still just the imagination at work: flimsy, ethereal, substance-less.

The two separate entities do not share the same story that has been passed on to them from their parents and grandparents. They are restricted and bound by the way they have each been taught by their own families, by the way they have been influenced and fashioned by their friends, and the friends of their friends, with all the prejudices and smallnesses and pockets of ignorance that we each learn, internalize, and then carry with us.

Although the two separate entities share, for some years, intersecting moments of the world's impartial chronology – the shared portion of a time-based Venn diagram – they do not share the same understanding of that moment. They have been presented to the world at a specific moment, but are separated by 40 years (or 30 years or 50 years) and are locked into that moment and separated from all others. This distance from each other exists despite the fact that most of us, as beings who are human, desire to comprehend other

THREE NOT VERY GOOD WOMEN

There have been lots of wicked people throughout history, including of course, during Roman times. In honour of my daughter (in case she thinks that only men can be bad) here are a few, all women (and all related, in some way or another, to the Emperor Claudius):

Valeria Messalina (c. 17/20 - 48 CE). As the third wife of the Emperor Claudius, she was at one point the most powerful woman in the Roman Empire. Ancient Roman sources portray Messalina as lustful, cruel and prone to debauchery of various sorts. Pliny the Elder wrote about a 24-hour competition that she had with a prostitute, to see who could take on the most partners. Messalina won with 25. She conspired against Claudius and was executed when the plot was uncovered. Claudius ordered that mention of her name was to be stricken from all documents, monuments and inscriptions. Despite that, Asteroid 545 Messalina is named for her.

Agostino Carracci (1557-1602) "Messaline Dans la Loge de Lisisca" (detail)

(According to "Against Women," Juvenal's sixth satire, Messalina worked in a brothel under the name Lycisca, "The Wolf-Girl.")

moments and other ways of processing the world's essential mysteries. This guesswork and speculation is healthy and inevitable for the most part, but it is still just guesswork and speculation.

I want to study Latin with my daughter because by doing so I can try to close the canyon gap between us, perhaps better navigate the quoggy spaces that thicken and congeal around us, and maybe even rewrite some of the lacuna that separates us. But the basis of my desire is to bring the two sides of the gap together, to recapture words of the lost manuscript, it is not to celebrate the seamless confluence of landscape or to revel in the effortless flow

Agrippina the Younger (15-59 CE). Ever on the lookout for nice women, Claudius then married Agrippina. Agrippina has been described as ruthless, violent and domineering by various classical sources. She schemed for years to gain the throne for her son, the future Emperor Nero, which included the poisoning of her husband, Claudius. As he grew more resentful of her power and influence, Nero began plotting her death. She survived one assassination attempt and as she was cornered by the soldiers who had been instructed to kill her, she thrust out her abdomen and screamed "Strike me here!" – the womb where she had carried her son. When news spread about the death of Agrippina, members of the Roman army and senate sent Nero letters of congratulations that he had succeeded in murdering his mother.

Sculpture of Agrippina crowning her young son, Nero

Locusta the Poisoner (d. 69 CE). Locusta has the distinction of being the first documented female serial killer. In 54 CE she was hired by Agrippina the Younger to poison Claudius, which was to be administered in a plate of mushrooms (the attempt failed). One year later, when Nero heard that she had been convicted of poisoning another person, he had the Praetorian Guards take her into custody. She was ordered to make a new potion to kill Claudius' son, Britannicus. She succeeded on her second try. Nero rewarded her with immunity while he lived, but seven months after Nero's suicide, she was executed by the Emperor Galba. One legend claims she was raped in public by a giraffe, after which she was torn apart by wild animals, but there is no documented evidence to support this claim.

Joseph-Noël Sylvestre (1847-1926) "Locusta Testing Poison on a Slave"

of words. This wish of mine, this want, is defined by the attempt to overcome a negative, not by the honouring of a positive.

Siobhan and I are, to put it simply, heading in opposite directions: the father is headed toward the past, infused with the memories of what he wanted to do and be, and attentive to the past memories of his child through the various stages of her life; the daughter is headed toward the future, where the world will open up and welcome her, will lead her to new discoveries and adventures, new potential. The father wants to reconstitute past connections and closeness (his version of personal antiquity), while the daughter wants the discovery of independence and freedom (her version of future terra incognita). In her magisterial book *Memoirs of Hadrian*, which I will refer to again in the closing pages, Marguerite Yourcenar writes about things "carried in different directions by two currents of time." There is, by definition, a mutual exclusivity built into these distinct father/daughter worldviews.

Throughout the Latin classics, we get expansive narratives and information about fathers and their sons, but very little about fathers and their daughters. The central image of the foundational text, Virgil's *Aeneid*, is Anchises (grandfather) and Aeneas (father) and Ascanius (son) fleeing Troy to become the founding ancestors of Rome. From Cicero, Seneca (both Elder and Younger), Pliny (both Elder and Younger) and many others, we read about connections between fathers and sons. We know that Quintilian, author of one of the most important texts on education that has ever been written, had a father who was interested in his education and that he had two sons, but he never mentions his mother or his wife, and we do not know whether he had any daughters.

From Catullus, Horace and Juvenal – who were either likely celibate or childless – we get constant commemorations of male friendship and camaraderie. In his "Epodes," for example, Horace talks about how "life is sweet" around his friend and patron Maecenas, and how "I will be less afraid if I am at your side." According to Suetonius, Maecenas made it clear in return how much affection he had for Horace:

> If I do not love you now, Horace,
> more than I love my own belly,
> I'd be thinner to look at than a hinny.

Also, again according to Suetonius, the Emperor Augustus teased his friend Horace by calling him "a very charming little man" and "a very perfect penis." Now that is what I would call male bonding!

FATHER VS. DAUGHTER VS. FATHER

Throughout Latin literature there is relatively little about fathers and their daughters, but there are some moments. Here, from the *Saturnalia* by Macrobius, are a few stories about the Emperor Augustus and his daughter, Julia:

"He told his friends that he had two spoiled daughters – the commonwealth and Julia – and he would just have to put up with them."

"She came to him dressed suggestively, and the sight offended her father, though he said nothing. The next day she changed her style of dress and, trying to look serious, gave her pleased father a hug. Though he had been able to conceal his unhappiness the day before, he couldn't conceal his joy now, and said, 'Isn't this style of dress so much more becoming in the daughter of Augustus'? But she was not at a loss for words in her own defense: 'Yes, because today I dressed to please my father; yesterday I dressed to please my husband'."

"Julia was getting prematurely grey and took to plucking her grey hair in secret. One day her father surprised her hairdressers with his arrival, and they stopped their work. Pretending not to notice the grey hairs on their garments, Augustus chatted about some other topics for a while before steering the conversation around to the topic of age, then asked his daughter whether – some years hence – she would rather be bald or grey: when she replied, 'I, father, would prefer to be grey', he reproved her fib by saying, 'Then why are these women trying so hard to make you bald'?"

Macrobius with his book.

In contrast, the basis for the most profound of all plays, *King Lear*, by the most important of all playwrights, William Shakespeare, is a disagreement between a father and his daughter, an inability for both father and daughter to see what is true before them. And it ushers forth some of Shakespeare's most violent language. "That she may feel / How sharper than a serpent's tooth it is / to have a thankless child" says Lear, as he invokes, with dragon-like anger, past, present and future pains.

Even in recent ages or our own age (presumably, we might think, more enlightened), when we would expect to get writing about fathers and daughters, there is very little. We get lots from the daughters (including various anthologies, and book-length offerings from Simone de Beauvoir, Margaret Salinger, Gwyneth Paltrow and many others), but very few from the father's perspective.

Linda Nielsen, a professor at Wake Forest University, is arguably the foremost authority on father-daughter relationships. Although once again we get the daughter's perspective rather than the father's, Nielsen is a strong advocate for more attention being paid to this area of research. As she says: "Fathers have a lifelong impact on their daughters, yet receive too little attention from educators, mental health and social service workers, and researchers." On one of her websites she offers a "Quiz," which includes the following questions and invites a true or false answer:

    ____   Fathers generally have less impact on their daughters than mothers do.

    ____   A daughter benefits more from a good relationship with mom than with dad.

    ____   Mothers know more than fathers about what's good for kids.

    ____   Fathers lack the natural instinct that mothers have for raising children.

    ____   Fathers have no natural instinct for taking care of infants the way that mothers do.

    ____   Mothers sacrifice more than fathers do for their children.

When respondents click on the link to get the right answers, this is what they read: "Not one of these statements is true based on recent social science research and national statistics." So there is some work to be done on this topic. And certainly there is room for men and fathers to contribute to the research.

Sometimes I think that perhaps the best thing for me to do is to realize how little I know about my daughter, and that it may always be like that. There are times when I think that I understand Siobhan pretty well and that this desire to study Latin alongside her is only adding to that solid under-pinning of knowledge. And then reality kicks in. I may say complimentary things endlessly –"You look cute today, Sweets." "I'm happy to help you study for your test, just let me know." "You have some really great friends." – and it seems as though Siobhan does not necessarily listen or respond. But if I happen to say one thing critical – "Sio-Sio, don't just throw the wet towel on the floor after you use it!" – that can come back to haunt me, with an exasperated "Dad!" or a grudging silence, or a complaint, I'm sure, to her friends via text message.

Once Siobhan and I were listening to a comedian on the radio, who told the following "joke":

> So my teenaged daughter comes home in a bit of a grumpy
> mood, and trying to cheer her up as she rushes past me, I ask
> her in a friendly voice "How was your day at school, honey?" She
> grunts, gives me the "death stare" and then goes into her bedroom
> and sends a few of her friends an email: "My Dad is such an
> asshole!" Using, of course, the fancy little laptop computer that I
> bought her last month!

I laughed with some familiarity at the joke, and Siobhan laughed with some sense of the inevitable.

As Dr. Leon Hoffman recently said in his blog "Beyond Freud" in *Psychology Today*, the relationships between fathers and their daughters can "turn on a dime." One moment, things seem fine, and the next there is a "tempestuous" daughter and an "angry and confused" father. Fathers and sons have much in common, but fathers, he says, have to "relate to their daughters in more complex ways." The average father may not even realize the source of their own discomfort, "he only knows that he is constantly being provoked by his daughter to reject her, to fight with her, or to ignore her."

During the fall, I was asked to drive Siobhan downtown to see a music concert with a few of her friends. Unlike previous times, this time there would be no parents to accompany the girls and stay with them during the concert.

"It'll be fun Dad," she says, as we drive downtown. "Although there'll probably be 'death circles' and people banging into each other."

"Umm ... 'death circles'? What is a 'death circle'?"

"Well it usually gets really cramped at the front – everyone is really packed so tight you can hardly move, you can hardly breathe. And then some guy, or a couple of guys, just start going crazy, start running into people, running at them and banging into them, to create a sort of space around them. They just bash into people until they have their own little space around them."

"So, you could get hurt pretty easy? Some moron could smash into you?"

"Ya, but you can kind of stay out of the way ... sometimes. But it's okay. It'll be fun."

"Are you sure? 'Death circles'! Yikes, and here I am dropping my daughter off to a world of 'death circles' and morons trying to knock other people over!"

Later, when we spoke about the concert, she mentioned that the bodies were so tightly packed together that they could hardly breathe: "If we all

LATIN GAMES

As a parent I have natural (although sometimes unfounded) concerns when my daughter and her friends participate in massive group activities, where things can get out of hand quickly and sometimes lead to violent ends. I'm thinking of massive music concerts, MMA fights, crowd rallies for political or other purposes, even sometimes large house parties when I don't have a direct knowledge of the parents or the kids who are "hosting" the party. Perhaps the concerns are unwarranted, but that does not lessen the state of worry. It is helpful, at least, to remember that in other times, things have been equally uncontrollable and raucous.

Rome, with a population of about a million, had the Circus Maximus, which had a capacity of 250,000! The site of chariot races, horse races, public games and festivals, the Circus Maximus easily dwarfs the largest stadiums we currently have anywhere in the world. During the races, four professional teams – Blue, Green, Red and White – vied for the honour and the tumultuous glory of winning. Marcus Aurelius, arguably one of the world's wisest philosopher-statesmen, on the first page of his *Meditations*, thanks his tutor for helping him to see the wisdom in not becoming a "Green or Blue supporter at the races." And Ovid, always with his mind on the ways of the flesh, thought that the circus was a great place to meet women because the seating wasn't segregated in the way it was in other theatres and amphitheatres around the city.

Julius Caesar once presented 320 pairs of gladiators to fight to the death. And Pompey, in his games, once presented for slaughter 20 elephants, 600 lions, 410 leopards, and the first rhinoceros ever seen in Rome. And Augustus – perhaps to consolidate the affections of the populace – decided to combine various group activities all on the same day: there was the hunting and slaughtering of wild beasts in the morning, around mid-day saw the public execution of low-status criminals, and then in the late afternoon there were the gladiatorial contests.

So when I consider the current entertainment options for my daughter, I have a certain measured sense of relative calm.

leaned at a 45-degree angle, no one would fall down. It was that tight. If the people on either side of me jumped at the same time, I would have been jumping too. And it's weird to watch the difference between groups and individual people. The individual people were fun and okay. But when they got into groups they could be really nasty. If a group of kids wanted to get to the front, near the stage, they would just bang into you and be really nasty, hitting you and stuff, just to get to where they wanted to get to. But it was fun Dad."

Yes, it certainly is true how little I know about my daughter and her daily life, which includes death circles, mosh pits, and whatever else the next crop of teenagers will invent to stir the blood. A couple of years ago, Siobhan emailed me a little joke she found on Facebook: "Guns don't kill people. Fathers with cute daughters kill people." There are times when I think that such wisdom may come in handy as she gets a bit older, and "boys" become part of the picture.

Sometimes I just have to accept that the conversations Siobhan and I have are strained and inconclusive, as they follow their own unique logic:

"Hey, Sio, take a look, here's the new umbrella I bought today. Pretty nice, eh?"

"What about the other one we had? The one we share? Why didn't you use it?"

"Looked everywhere. Couldn't find it."

"Ummm. It's in my backpack. Or maybe it's in my locker at school."

"The one we share?"

"Ya, the one we share."

"Well then how are we supposed to share it if it's in your locker?"

"Well."

"How can I use it if you have it?"

"I don't know."

"Ah … same here. I don't know."

"Me neither."

"Yep, me neither."

There's no sense continuing the conversation when these types of father-daughter interactions have such tautological perfection.

Of course in the midst of my multitudinous concerns about Siobhan's future, and my fears that she may yet become the hellion (a word my mom once used to describe one of my sisters) that some of my friends who are fellow-parents say is sure to happen, I often tell stories to myself and others about how well Siobhan and I get along. I also brag about her to friends and family. But is that just a series of self-deluding stories? Is there anything in my observations that have any staying power? Do I tell great things about Siobhan because that is simply what I want to say and because that is simply what I want to hear? Of course I have fond memories of some great times that we have spent together, but does this have any real influence on how she may be ten years or twenty years from now?

When it comes to their kids, parents see danger everywhere. I wonder, of course, how best to help Siobhan scull the hitherandthithering waters of adolescence. As *National Geographic* recently stated in an article called "The New Science of the Teenage Brain": "The United States spends about a billion dollars a year on programs to counsel adolescents on violence, gangs, suicide, sex, substance abuse, and other potential pitfalls." The magazine then completed the thought: "Few of them work."

In the midst of a teen's natural inclination to learn from their peers, the magazine said that parents have to know when and where to provide a bit of insight, what it called "certain kernels of wisdom – knowledge valued not because it comes from parental authority but because it comes from the parent's own struggles to learn how the world turns." Fortunately for Siobhan, I have experienced, as most people have, my own share of these struggles. I never had much personal experience with drugs or drinking, although I certainly witnessed them in my large family and through my high school and university years. But I do have some wisdom to offer Siobhan about relationship struggles, money struggles, and about my personal favourite struggle: what-am-I-going-to-do-when-I-grow-up? And Siobhan has seen signs of real conflict within and among her extended family – uncles, aunts, and other relatives on both the paternal and maternal sides of her family who have gone through trying, dangerous and self-destructive acts. There's enough there to teach her, should she want to learn, a few lessons about the results of wayward behaviour, bad luck, unbottled anger, poor life choices, and the short- and long-term costs of these things.

My specific fears and questions about Siobhan's future sometime seem to take up more room, more oxygen, than my celebrations of her past achievements. And my fears are both large and small. Will she remain healthy as she starts to age? Will her self-confidence, never a particularly strong suit for most teenaged girls, find its own permanent footing? Will she continue to be surrounded by smart and intelligent and fun friends? Will she find work that fulfills and pleases her? Will she have the fortitude to deal with the difficulties and challenges and tragedies that will certainly be part of her future? Will her later teenage years take on a sullen, angry flavour, which seems to be expected by many of my friends? "Oh, she's 14! Watch out!" they say. "Here come the teenage years – I hope you survive them." "Good luck for the next five years." I get many more ominous

THESE ARE A FEW OF MY NOT FAVOURITE THINGS

Consumer-saturated celebrity fashion and moshing/death circles and whatever their inevitable successors turn out to be.

comments from my friends who have teenaged girls than I do reassuring ones.

Over the years I have heard of a wide range of teenage problems from people I know. One friend talks about her daughter's "pre-drinking" – that is, drinking for free at home out of the family liquor cabinet before she goes out drinking with her friends. Another friend has spoken to me about his daughter's eating disorders and the medical intervention required. Yet another told me about his daughter's sudden change of temperament. Of how one day she was quite comfortable in her own skin, doing well at school, and had lots of friends. And then, all of a sudden, for some reason or reasons, she started cutting herself and doing drugs of various sorts, and packing condoms in her purse whenever she went out. And all this happened when she was 13 and 14. The family ended up taking her out of school and travelling for six months as a way of breaking the habits that she had developed. They do not yet know whether the family commitment to help her has had any positive influence on her.

Of course in our Internet-saturated age, the problems of sexting and other compromising online behaviour has a staying power unknown to previous generations. In a recent magazine article, "My Cybersexual Education," Alexandra Molotkow traces her "cybersex, hookups with strangers and other tales of growing up online." Although she provides some historical context by noting that kids "have ruined their own lives for millennia, through any medium they can master," Molotkow also says, "My generation has left an excruciatingly detailed record of the process of growing up." She also highlights recent research: how one American study found that 20 percent of teens have sent compromising photos of themselves to other kids or posted them on the Internet, and how 42 percent of 10- to 17-year-olds had seen porn online in the past year.

According to NetFamilyNews.org, one of the most respected resources for families seeking information about web safety and security, there are about 250 million sexually explicit web pages across all top level domain names. That's a lot of pornography, and it's very easy to access. And a recent study by the Crimes Against Children Research Centre at the University of

New Hampshire found that one in seven kids had received sexual advances online.

Any parent who is not worried about these statistics, who is not frightened by the current and long-term effects of these activities, is living with their analog head stuck unknowingly in the digital sand.

So not only do I not know about my daughter's inner landscape, about many of the formative influences on her, about how she processes and learns from the people and influences around her, I'm not sure I'll ever have the ability to know these things. As I read a few articles and stories about women talking about their fathers I see that there are whole worlds that are completely foreign to me – that there are ways of thinking that I cannot hope to approach even if I wanted to.

In the pieces gathered in the collections *The First Man in My Life: Daughters Write About Their Fathers* and *What My Father Gave Me: Daughters Speak,* one of the daughters hires a private detective to search out news of an absent father (writer Camilla Gibb). In another, written by a "myth-dispelling" daughter, we get the background observations as she follows her father with "clear-eyed anticipation of Dad's nerves and Scotch-fuelled barf" (Emma Richler, writing about her father, Mordecai Richler). And in another we get the memories of a father that are fuelled by a "pilot light of pure hatred" (writer Saleema Nawaz).

As the writer and editor Melanie Little says, talking about her father: "I watched him, studied him, to get a better sense of me. Who I was, what was I like, where did I fit." The writer Susan Swan says that if she had sent a letter to her father a few years ago she would have written something like this: "Dear Dad. Thanks a lot, you narcissistic son of a bitch, for ignoring me most of my childhood and giving all your time to your patients instead of your family." She then goes on to say that if she sent the same letter now, she might say: "Dear Dad: Why has it taken me all these years to see you as a person? And to understand that your reasons for working so hard as a country doctor had nothing to do with me?"

VOCABULARY CHECKLIST

anxiety – n. anxietas

confusion – n. confusio

friend – n. amicus

ignorance – n. inscientia

knowledge – n. scientia

PRACTICING THE LANGUAGE

Learning to cope with challenges is part of growing up.
Ut homo prudens fias necesse est aerumnis naviter resistere.

How is any father, how am I, supposed to be able to navigate through this land of colours and shapes that I have never seen before? This topography that presents me with hidden shoals and darkened caves and flint-like edges that I have never experienced myself? This Daughterland that defines itself only as it passes by, and does not come with its own guidebook?

Perhaps the best that I can do is to realize how little I know and how little I'll ever know about Siobhan and her circuitous affections, inducements and hungers.

Of course even when we know it is either foolish or dangerous, most parents still want to know more about what goes on in the minds of our kids. This is especially true when kids reach the teenaged years and all of a sudden they are not as forthcoming or as direct or as playfully connected to us as they used to be.

There are lots of ways for these parental worries to manifest themselves, some based on good and some based on not-good speculation. Everything from the benign "Is my kid okay?" or "What can I do to help/ assist/encourage my kid?" to "What am I supposed to do when I want to talk but my kid does not?" and "Is my son/daughter quiet because he/she is depressed?" and "Are they sullen because they hate us?" and "Do they hate us because they are smarter than we are?" and "Are they smarter than us because they know who and when to hate?" and … well you get the idea. The questions sometimes lead down dead ends and sometimes only cause more trouble than they resolve.

In his book *Rome*, Robert Hughes quotes an Italian official confronted by the 19th-century politician and activist Giuseppe Mazzini, nicknamed the "Soul of Italy." The official told Mazzini's father: "Your son is a man of some talent, and he is too fond of walking by himself at night deep in thought. What on earth has he to think about at his age? We do not like young people to think unless we know the subject of their thoughts." This is a similar statement to what Julius Caesar says in the eponymous Shakespeare play, when he talks about Cassius: "He thinks too much: such men are dangerous."

Now I'm not advocating such an unattainable and destructive position – of wanting to know all that goes on in the mind of Siobhan – but sometimes, just sometimes, I wish I had a greater insight into the workings of her thoughts, and that is probably not unusual for most parents as they contemplate the emotional comings and goings of their children. There are, as parents know, some bad things out there. Perhaps if we had the opportunity to pass on some of our "wisdom" about these bad things to our kids – some benefit of our experience – it might alleviate some of the disconnection and confusion that rests unseen in the tangled gardens and threatening wildlife that await our kids.

Who knows? They may even appreciate the gesture, may find some insight in such parental "knowledge." They may even thank us, at some point. Although, probably more likely, not.

CHAPTER SEVEN

THE ETERNAL UGLY

"… they stumbled over the stumbling stone …"
Romans 9:33

"Stop quoting laws at us! We're the ones wearing swords!"
Plutarch, *Pompey*

HAS THERE EVER BEEN an age other than ours when the fuse of civilization has been so short – when we have been so connected to complete and utter collapse? How could there have been?

As I wander among the Latin classics and study alongside my daughter I do, of course, have moments of pleasure and optimism. But absorbing and processing the swirling windstorm

THE UGLY

Head of a man, from the Glypothek, Munich.

of news and information that howls everywhere around us – on TV, in the newspapers, among the multitude of laneways and superhighways that make up the cosmorama of the Internet – I worry, like any parent, about the world we are leaving to our children. I worry that Siobhan will be saddled with the wrongs of our generation and that of previous generations. I worry that her generation will simply be so constricted by the fallout of past mistakes – the shortsightedness, or blindness, that seems so much a part of what it means to be human – that it will not be able to reach its full potential. I worry that the information we give and the lessons that we teach our children may not be the ones that allow them to succeed – as people and creators and innovators. But has it ever been different?

As I've been trying to understand the ways that Siobhan sees the world, and thinking about the early Latin writers, I've gained a little learning (a dangerous thing, to be sure) of history and its eternal, cyclical nature. It's not much of an insight, but here is one that I've come to: Other than every other moment of human existence, has there ever been an era more dictated by stupidity and ignorance and superstition than our own? Put another way: In our era we are defined by our abundant stupidities, ignorance and superstitions, but has it ever been otherwise?

The debate as to whether our civilization is in collapse or not, and what our current models should be, is a constant drum roll among historians, social commentators and pundits of all sorts, and has been for some time. The 85 essays that make up the Federalist Papers – written by James Madison, Alexander Hamilton and John Jay (collectively writing under the pseudonym "Publius") in support of the ratification of the U.S. constitution – read like an ongoing debate on the benefits and inadequacies of the Romans and their fledgling policies. When the proposed constitution was sent to the Confederation Congress, which then submitted it to the states for ratification, it became the target of many articles in the press written by opponents writing under such names as "Cato" and "Brutus." William Duer later would write in support of the three Federalist authors under the name "Philo-Publius," or "Friend of Publius." Madison, Hamilton and Jay are, of course, all Founding Fathers, and Duer was one of the signers of the Articles of Confederation.

Early Americans are not the only ones who have debated the examples – good, bad and ugly – left to us by the Romans. English author, satirist and morals campaigner Malcolm Muggeridge was one of the most strident. "The basic condition for a civilization," he wrote, "is that there should be law and order." And then he went on:

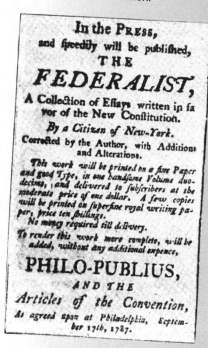

> Obviously this is coming to an end. The world is falling into chaos, even perhaps especially our western world. ... There are many other symptoms. The excessive interest in eroticism is characteristic of the end of a civilization because it really means a growing impotence, and fear of impotence. Then the excessive need for excitement, vicarious excitement, which of course the games provided for the Romans and which television provides for our population. Even the enormously complicated structure of taxation and administration is a symptom of the end of the civilization. Above all, there is this truly terrible thing which afflicts materialistic societies – boredom, an excessive boredom which I note on every hand.

The recently deceased Gore Vidal, in his book *The Decline and Fall of the American Empire*, and elsewhere, considered that he was presiding over the end of American civilization. And the list of commentators (doomsayers mostly, but some are sanguine) goes on. The two books that most recently seem to have galvanized the argument in its most complex and multifaceted form both use the word "Rome" in their titles.

In *Are We Rome? The Fall of an Empire and the Fate of America*, Cullen Murphy presents an intelligent picture of the connections of the two "empires" and asks a series of germane and provocative questions: "Does the fate of Rome tell us anything useful about America's present or America's future? Must decline and fall lurk somewhere ahead? Can we learn from Rome's mistakes? Take heart from Rome's achievements? And by the way, what exactly *was* the fate of the Roman Empire?" When Walter Isaacson, the biographer of Steve Jobs, reviewed Murphy's book for *The New York Times* he referenced the "fat, flabby and unwieldy" nature of the declining Rome, and how "fixers, flatterers and bureaucrats" clung to power. Sounds familiar, no? Isaacson also spoke of the exceptionalism, patronage and protectionism that hindered and weakened the two empires.

A HANDY ENDING

The end is always, of course, at hand. Such thoughts help us to focus on the present. A photograph I took in November 1977, in London, England.

In *Why America Is Not a New Rome*, Vaclav Smil provides a counterbalance to what he calls "facile comparisons" between the two "empires." As he says, "a systematic appraisal of fundamental realities exposes truly profound differences that make casual comparisons of the two empires at best misplaced but more often irrelevant. Understanding this is important – important in order to avoid misleading parallels, and important in order to look ahead without the burden of false and counterproductive analogies." When Bill Gates, the founder of Microsoft (and who also studied Latin), reviewed Smil's book on his blog, www.thegatesnotes.com, he noted: "It is certainly interesting to discuss how the U.S. position will change in the future, but reaching back to Roman analogies will not aid in that discussion. Most references to Rome simply talk about things that are common to all large and long-lasting governments – complexity, disagreement, and some level of failed ambition."

So how am I, a parent of a teenaged girl who is simultaneously exploring the ancient world and steeped in contemporary technology, to provide some guidance, some objective wisdom to her? Perhaps the best way, the only way, is to let her seek and discover these things – with all their links and rifts – for herself. Sometimes these tactics of seeking and discovering have a certain banal humour to them. Here is a conversation we had on a mid-winter morning in December:

"How cold is it outside, Dad?"

"Pretty warm today. Look at the sun just screaming in through the windows. It looks nice."

"Can you check on your iPhone?"

"Sure … okay … it says it will be about 5 degrees today, and lots of sun."

"Should I wear my pea coat or the puffy one with down in it?"

"I don't know, Poops. You decide."

"Well, I don't have my pea coat. It's at Mom's. So I'll wear the down coat."

"Sounds good."

"Will I need my hat?"

"Probably not."

"Will I need my gloves?"

"No, not really."

"What about a scarf?'

"Ummm."

"Dad, do I look fat in this down coat? It really puffs up."

"Nope. I think it looks good. And everyone knows that it's a puffy down coat, so I think people will say you look skinny in it."

"Really?"

"Sure. Why not? I think you look cute in it."

"OK."

"Are you gonna be warm enough, without a hat or gloves or scarf?"

"Sure, I think so."

"OK."

"OK."

At other times the conversations take on a tug-of-war flavour, where sometimes there are two "winners" (that is, information actually gets exchanged) but sometimes there is just a circular stalemate. In mid-January, conversations about boys started taking on more urgency, as a few of Siobhan's friends started to acquire boyfriends. We started to talk, from time to time, about things that we had never talked about before, and used words that we had never used before, including various activities that boys and girls have been known to participate in! For a father, these first few conversations are a shock. ("Yikes! Did I just use that word?" "How does my sweet little daughter know about that?" "Do all teens these days talk like this?") In our case, I think it was more uncomfortable for me than it was for Siobhan. Here is one of the

AN INSCRIPTION THAT COULD BE WRITTEN TODAY

"Some time ago an archaeologist in the Near East dug up an inscription five thousand years old which told him that 'children no longer obey their parents, and the end of the world is rapidly approaching'."

— Northrop Frye

tamer, stalemate conversations (with an editorial gloss on intonations and emotions) that we had soon after the "boy" conversations started:

"So what about your friend ... the one with the new boyfriend?" (Inquisitive, with a slight needling tone.)

"Dad!" (With a nervous grin and a small roll of the eyes.)

"Well, any news?" (An inquiry halfway between prodding and playful.)

"Dad!" (More emphatic this time. A sense of exasperation. More of a jaw-drop than a grin.)

"Well?" (Slightly desperate. I'm beginning to realize that this conversation is really not going anywhere.)

"Dad, do we have to talk about this now?" (A tone somewhere between "you're-being-weird" and "why-are-you-bugging-me?")

"OK, OK, I won't push it." (One last attempt at reverse psychology: maybe if I pretend not to care, she'll start to talk ...)

"Good!" (Relief. A timbre of "that-is-the-end-of-this-conversation" mixed with a strong sense of "I-control-these-conversations-and-will-only-talk-about-this-stuff-when-I-want-to.")

"OK. It's fine with me!" (Ah well, I lost another one ...)

The main thing, I keep telling myself, is to allow her the space to find things out for herself and to make her own mistakes. Is there really, I say to myself in those rare moments of lucidity, any other way to learn? And a large part of this learning – we are talking, after all, about teenagers – has to come through exploration, as well as fun, adventure, and play. Teens try things out, they test themselves, they push the personal and societal boundaries that they sense around them. We are all, parents and kids alike, as Johan Huizinga says, *homo ludens* – "people at play" – so why fight it? Such playful activities depend on tactics that change over the years and millennia, but they are always with us. The technology changes, but the impulse remains. One of Siobhan's touchstones (although she may not use that word) is "Just Breathe." There is a quite an accepting wisdom in that.

Let's face it: Many of us have perhaps too much time, and too much of an inclination, to lament the state of our lives, the state of the union and the state of the world. Wars, infidelities, political stalemates, home-grown terrorists, borrowed credit, apathetic youth – there's a lot to choose from.

ETERNAL INSULTS AND INVECTIVE

Throughout literature and politics, there are nasty insults and cruel put-downs, many of them either within a creative work (think of Shakespeare's metaphoric insults) or meant to be pseudo-private comments from one person to another (think of Oscar Wilde or Winston Churchill).

The Death of Cicero, from a 15th-century manuscript

Cicero, the greatest orator of the ancient world, wrote and recited his insults, his invective, for the public and for posterity. Here he is taking on Mark Antony in one of his greatest speeches, *Second Philippic*, as translated by D. H. Berry. The fact that he was murdered within the year for writing the *Philippics* demonstrates, perhaps, that there has been ample ugliness among us for millennia. (After his murder, on Antony's orders, Cicero's head and hands – that had composed and written the *Philippics* – were cut off and publicly displayed in Rome; Fulvia, Antony's wife, is said to have mutilated Cicero's head and tongue after his murder.) In this speech, Cicero calls Antony or references his

"pretty-boy looks"
"an enemy of his country"
"worn out with wine and fornication, you daily indulged … in every type of perversion"
"look at his astonishing stupidity"
"I thereby prove you guilty not just of bad manners, but of madness"
"What scandalous disgrace, what intolerable cheek, wickedness, and depravity!"
"You despicable wretch."

"his stupidity – a quality in which he surpasses everyone else"

"you utter moron"

"consider the doziness of this man – this sheep, rather"

"Sleep off your drunkenness, I tell you; belch it out!"

"you utter lunatic"

"you criminal"

"you were a common prostitute" (i.e. you prostituted yourself to other men, and took the dishonourable passive [female] role, in Berry's words)

"the root of all our troubles sprang from the man's wickedness"

"the enemy of this state"

"the bringer of pestilence and death"

"He drenched himself in the blood of citizens"

"a lightweight kind of worthlessness"

"he vomited, filling his lap ... with morsels of food stinking of wine!"

"so treacherous, so insane, so hostile to the gods and mankind"

"an object of detestation"

"crazed and violent"

"wastrel"

"What a worthless individual!"

"a man who is never sober!"

"Was any flunky ever so subservient, so groveling?"

"scoundrel"

"Are you in your right mind? Should you not be in a straightjacket?"

In this one speech Cicero also accuses Antony of forgery, illegal gambling, theft of property and money (from individuals and from the state), being a childhood bankrupt, adultery, attempted murder, murder, being the cause of the civil war between Caesar and Pompey, the slaughterer of three armies of Roman soldiers, being guilty of religious crimes, annulling legally enacted laws and wills, marketing himself as worthy of praise, and addressing a public meeting in the nude.

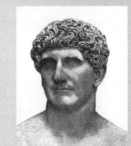

"Pretty-boy" Mark Antony

Perhaps it is both wise and comforting to take a very deep breath, or a few, and remember that we have seen similar societal, political and economic tumult before, and more-or-less survived.

The Roman era brought us the elegant and delightful wisdom of Virgil and Ovid, and classic architecture that still stands and impresses. But it also brought us government waste on a massive scale, gluttony and gambling of epic proportions, every type of sexual excess, notions of exceptionalism and international bravado that has brought on intractable wars, as well as pan-handling, mud-wrestling and graffiti.

You may think that infantile or idiotic entertainments dominate our lives now, but the three-tiered Circus Maximus, which I mentioned earlier, the home to jugglers, fortune tellers, plays and horse races, could hold one-quarter of Rome's 1,000,000 citizens! Festivals and Ludi, the public games put on to entertain the population and keep their minds off hunger, political corruption and the staggering costs of war in the provinces, sometimes occupied 180 days of the year. At least one of the festivals, the Ludi Plebeii, went on for 14 days straight. And let's not forget that the Colosseum opened around 80 CE with a gladiatorial spectacle lasting 100 days.

Are you worried that our age is overrun by violence and senseless wars? Afghanistan, Syria, Ukraine, et cetera. Plutarch reminds us that after one civil war battle in northern Italy the corpses were piled higher than the eagle standards (maybe 10-12 feet), because of course in Roman civil wars no prisoners were taken. And in 71 BCE, Marcus Crassus, in celebrating his victory over the slave revolt led by Spartacus, crucified 6,000 slaves along the Appian Way between Rome and Capua. (The execution of 6,000 people on a well-travelled road – now that sends a message!)

Maybe you are worried about the recurrent rash of piracy off the coast of Somalia that threatens vital international shipping routes. Various Roman historians remind us that during the height of the Roman Empire there were perhaps 20,000 pirates in the Mediterranean, and their presence was so pervasive that the sea was often all but closed to commercial traffic.

For staggering government-sanctioned waste and sexual extravagances that make recent scandals involving Toronto Mayor Rob Ford and other twerps like him wither in comparison, read Suetonius on the "insolence, lust, luxury, and greed" of Nero, or on the "appalling deeds" and "shamelessness" of Caligula, or on the "ingenious and unpredictable" cruelty of Domitian. For an all-consuming exceptionalism, read Cicero as he describes himself and his home city of Rome in his famed speeches against Catiline, especially where he documents his "unambiguous signs from the immortal gods, under whose guidance I have arrived." For an update on the scale of gambling and gluttony and cross-dressing and witchcraft 2,000 years ago, don't miss Horace and Apuleius and Ovid.

And to reassure yourself that obsessing over fashion really has never gone out of fashion, read Seneca the Elder and his comments on "the luxury of this generation" which has led, it seems, to "idle" and "sluggish" youth who seem to care only for "sleep and apathy" and the need to "crimp their hair" and spend all their time "grooming themselves."

For scatological and sexual insults that are breathtaking in their crudeness – and that make the *Jackass*, *Hangover* and

EXTREME GLUTTONY

During the height of the Roman Empire, gluttony became more and more outrageous. Some particularly wealthy citizens sat on chairs of solid silver, ate with solid gold utensils, and dined on elephant ears and lamprey milk. According to the historian Suetonius, the Emperor Vitellius once offered at one of his grand feasts "two thousand of the choicest fish and seven thousand birds." On one dinner platter Vitellius "blended the livers of scar-fish, the brains of pheasants and peacocks, the tongues of flamingoes, and the innards of lampreys." Often the meals were immediately expelled, in the vomitorium – sometimes with a slave using a long feather to induce the process – which efficiently made room for yet more gorging.

A big bust, indeed. The Emperor Vitellius, from the Louvre.

Bridesmaids movies seem downright docile – you really can't do much better than Catullus, although Martial's epigrams come close. (Sorry, you'll have to seek out those abundantly licentious and excretory quotations for yourself.)

All of this is, of course, to say nothing of tumult in Libya (see CNN or Virgil's *Aeneid*), and the troubles with Greece (follow the IMF website or read Plautus's comedies), and that small chunk of land on the eastern edge of the Mediterranean that seems to be constantly at war within itself and with its neighbours (read *The Jerusalem Post* or *The Annals* by Tacitus).

Intertwined with and fixated on our own time and space, we may find some solace in recalling that the frivolities and violences of our age were present, in abundance, in other ages. Two thousand years ago Juvenal documented the "thousand risks of this terrible city," Rome, which included public belching, the stench of body odour, traffic-jams, muggings in the streets, inflation, and living beyond our means on borrowed money. And Tacitus, acknowledged as the last major writer of classical Latin prose, said Rome was "where all that is abominable and shameful in the world flows together and gains popularity."

Perhaps the best advice there is to help you enjoy your life, especially if your thoughts and worries bring on unbidden concerns about the troubling state of our current world, is to relax. We've seen this sort of stuff before. And we've survived. Just Breathe.

We are not coming to the end of civilization. Although the formal elements of the Roman Empire came to an end, and elements of Western civilization went dormant for some time, civilization continued. The Romans' language lives on to this day, in a multitude of forms and in high schools and universities in Munich, London, New York, Paris, Toronto and many other cities around the world. Roman wisdom on democracy lives on. The elegant and combative words of Cicero live on, as do the lessons and writings of that colossus, Julius Caesar.

It also does us well to remember that ancient Roman thinkers and writers complained about the same things that we complain about. They worried about (and lived through) wars among nations as well as a series of civil wars. And experienced (and thought about) inflation, contraception, slavery, book burning, government corruption, the rich vs. the poor, drug use, greed, religious orthodoxy and religious fanaticism, family succession and diet fads. Pick your favourite topic – it is all found in the Latin literature from two millennia ago. Perhaps there is some comfort to be derived here: this is simply the way it has always been and there's no sense in endlessly wishing that the world was otherwise.

In a strange way, it may be healthy that we constantly think that we are at the end of times, that we are in a state of inevitable collapse, that we are about to experience the end of our lives. (Eschatology – it's a "game" that has been played since before Homer and the Bible, and that everyone still seems quite pleased to go on playing. And let's not forget rampant "Apocaholism," which Matt Ridley intones in his encouraging book *The Rational Optimist*.) If we can prevent such feelings from completely incapacitating us, perhaps they can help us focus and direct our attention. Siobhan, like all teenagers, has an incredible desire to move forward, to try to figure out what is going to happen next, to anticipate tomorrow's activities. By studying Latin, and by exploring a sense of history, she is also able to realize that there is a dynamic past at work that is always helping to shape a protean present and fungible future. That the world always simultaneously concerns itself with the past, the present and the future. That there is an eternality to the world, and to our imaginations. There are ugly elements of our world, to be sure, but we've managed to keep moving forward, despite our faults and inadequacies. A sense of history, of how things have moved from there to here, from Latin to English, from way back then to right now, is a good thing for any person to have, especially a teenager.

When Siobhan was about eight or nine we used to read a great book for kids called *The Horrible History of the World*. It's colourful, lively, fun, and highlights the despicable ways of Herod, Attila the Hun, Torquemada, and Hitler, among many others. Somehow we managed to be both shocked and entertained by the gruesome stories and the blood-dripping drawings.

Is the Roman Empire like our era? Are we destined to repeat those ugly habits and self-immolating tendencies? Is our era in its "decline and fall" stage? Of course there are no answers to these inevitable and eternal questions. Many elements of the world are less than appealing … but it has always been thus. And I find some curious solace in all this questioning. Perhaps the world I am leaving to Siobhan, the world we are all leaving to our kids – equal parts hopelessness and potential, despair and joy – is exactly the sort of world that we should be leaving to them. Human nature being what it is, we don't really have much of a choice anyway.

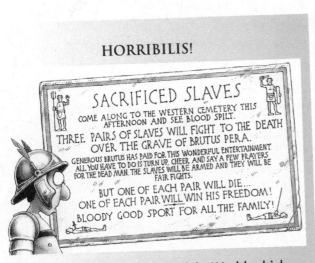

HORRIBILIS!

From *The Horrible History of the World*, which Siobhan and I both found rather endearing.

In his engaging biography of Cicero, historian Anthony Everitt provides a very efficient perspective on this whole question of how similar or dissimilar we are to the Romans. He notes "first, how unrecognizably different a world the Roman Republic was from ours, and, second, that the motives of human behaviour do not change." That seems to me a very sensible way to see the supposed distinctions and similarities between the Romans and ourselves: many of the details (political organizations, family structures, creative outlets) are different, but many of the basics (political instincts, family affections, creative impulses) are the same. That is an appropriate and reasonable way for me and Siobhan to see this excellent adventure, this transporting flourish of history in which we find ourselves.

And, really, have we changed that much since the Stone Age? As Matt Ridley states, talking about such trust-based sites as eBay and Wikipedia:

"Perhaps the Internet has returned us to a world a bit like the Stone Age in which there is no place for a fraudster to hide." Or, more pointedly, here is Kate Fox, a social anthropologist and a director of the Social Issues Research Centre in Oxford, England: "Our brains haven't changed since the Stone Age, and humans are designed to live in small groups in which everyone knows one another. Google is an attempt to recreate a primeval, pre-industrial pattern of interaction."

VOCABULARY CHECKLIST

civilization – n. cultus

eternal – adj. aeternus

fashion – n. modus

gossip – n. (person) homo garrulus

we – pn. nos

PRACTICING THE LANGUAGE

The world has a way of repeating itself.

Nescio quomodo res nostrae se identidem iterant.

CHAPTER EIGHT

TECHNOLOGY WILL SET YOU FREE!

"Silly, or downright disastrous, are all the things that we pray for."
Juvenal, *The Tenth Satire*

"If you follow nature, you will not need technology."
Seneca, *Epistle 90*

SOMETIMES, WHEN I HAVE NOT RECEIVED AN EMAIL for a while (say, 20 minutes or so) I send an email to myself, just to check if the all-knowing cloud and the local, international and extra-terrestrial server farms, satellites and other technological paraphernalia are still functioning, still capable of remembering me and my specific email address, still interested in showing me a little love. The pathetic thing is that, a moment later, when that pleasant Pavlovian beep from my iPhone sounds, telling me I have received an email, I get excited and instantly check my inbox. My thoughts go something like: "Ha! The world remembers me! Joy! Rapture!" And then I check, and see the email I've just sent myself, at which point my thoughts proceed: "Sad. Very sad. Dumb. Very dumb."

Siobhan, of course, has an innate and instinctual understanding of technology – its multitude of services, pleasures and uses. She has her Facebook account, as well as her Hotmail account, and has put stuff out to the world on YouTube, and through Twitter, Tumblr, Flickr and a host of other sites that depend on user-generated content.

I once asked her if she had ever done something so pitiful as send herself an email, heard that cheerful ping telling her that she had received an email, then checked her account only to realize that ... well, you get the idea. "Oh yeah, Dad, I've done that. Sometimes I'll be in Facebook, send myself a copy of an article or send myself a reminder about something I have to do, then hear the beep, check my email and realize ... ah, kinda pathetic ... did I really just forget that I just sent myself an email?! ... Sure, Dad, probably most people have done that."

You cannot imagine the relief I get when I talk with my techno-daughter about my self-inflicted digital stupidities and hear that she too has such weaknesses and misplaced excitements.

Siobhan is a truly wired kid. She has, at the moment, very close connections to eight screens: her iPod, her cellphone, her iPad, her own netbook, my laptop computer, her mom's desktop computer, and TVs at both her parents' houses. This is not, of course, counting the screens and monitors at her school, the devices that her friends have and that she might use (just as her friends sometimes use her devices), and the flickering electronic portals that are on the subway, in stores, and that hover attentively above the streets and highways that transect and encircle every industrialized city around the world. These days, all of us – from fresh infants who have every grimace and drool recorded by digital cameras to failing centenarians who at the end of their days have their every heartbeat and brainwave monitored by hospital screens that beep and flicker – are integrated with, surrounded by, and consummated by technology.

We should not forget, however, that language itself is a technology, an invention. It was created, as all technologies over the years have been, through experimentation and trial and error, and it is constantly morphing and adapting. As and Bs and Cs took a long time to get to us in their current form. Humans invent things and use technologies – we always have and we always will. The tools that we have created (language, the wheel, particle accelerators) are what distinguish us and how we define ourselves.

Technologies – whether we mean grunting out a guttural, repeatable sound that can be understood by our fellow cave-dwellers to mean "food," or whether we're adapting massively multiplayer online virtual words to help sequence human DNA – are both mirrors and windows. They reflect back to our inquisitive faces everything that we see around us and everything that we want to see around us. They dissolve the diaphanous barriers that separate us from the world and thus fool us into thinking that the frames that border and restrict our personal vision have dissolved

THE TECHNOLOGY THAT ENABLES MANY OTHER TECHNOLOGIES

Our most important technology, represented here by scratches on a large black piece of granite. These symbols and letters (ancient Egyptian hieroglyphics, Demotic and ancient Greek) on the Rosetta Stone, and others like them that we have developed over the millennia, allow us to communicate with each other.

into the ether. And they provide opportunities, breaths of fresh air, that we may not have experienced before.

In his book of charming bewilderments, *The Story of Language*, Mario Pei talks about the still unsolved origins of human speech, including the "bow-wow," "ding-dong," "pooh-pooh" and "ta-ta" theories. Silly names perhaps, but Pei is utterly compelling in his expansive historical assessment of how languages were invented and how the great technologies we know as alphabets came to be created.

These days there are many who believe that the Internet (to use a catch-all word for our wired existence) is making us more facile, more ignorant. Neil Postman in his seminal 1985 book *Amusing Ourselves to Death: Public Discourse in the Age of Show Business* helped start this most recent round of discussion of how technology is the main deadening agent of our intelligence and our soul. Nicholas Carr, Chris Hedges and Sherry Turkle are three among many who have written subsequent books on the topic.

I've had various conversations over the years with friends (some who have articulate things to say about a wide range of topics), who are convinced that technology is doing us much more harm than good, and that kids who are growing up now will be the worse because of this all-consuming technology, this voracious swarm of ones and zeros that eats everything in its path. I never use the phrase "technological eschatologist" in these conversations (it is way too clunky and multisyllabic) but I do use this phrase in my own internal conversations to describe people I know who are convinced that current technology is beginning to usher in the end of the world, that current technology is beginning the process of making us all slower, simpler and more stupid.

THE MEDIUM DOES NOT ALWAYS NEED A MESSAGE

"One of the pleasures of digital communication is that it does not need a message. It can be there to trigger a feeling rather than transmit a thought. Indeed, for many teenagers who discover their feelings by texting them, communication is the place where feelings are born."
— Sherry Turkle

How can I believe this dire forecast when I have a teenaged daughter? Is it willful ignorance, a suspension of my own belief system, to not accept that things will be worse for Siobhan than previous generations? Shouldn't I just accept that the world is being destroyed by technology? Is Nicholas Carr correct when he says in *The Shallows: What the Internet is Doing to Our Brains* that the Internet and the offloading of memory to external data banks "doesn't just threaten the depth and distinctiveness of the self. It threatens the depth and distinctiveness of the culture we all share"?

It has become somewhat of a cliché for people concerned about the ravages of technology to quote Marshall McLuhan's famous phrase: "We shape our tools and thereafter our tools shape us." But of course, this has always been true, for better or ill, of all of our technologies: from the first rough roads traversing what we now call North Africa (where it may have taken eight months to travel from Carthage to Ethiopia), to the Mars rover, Curiosity (which took eight months to get from Earth to the red planet). McLuhan also understood that technology – he tended to use the words tool, media, medium and technology almost interchangeably – is also a metaphor. He could just have easily said: "Our tools shape us, but it is we who shape the tools." To state the obvious: the human imagination is only capable of shaping tools that we ourselves want and choose to shape. We build tools that enable birth and death – conception and killing – because that's what we want to do. We are our tools, we are our technology – and it has always been thus.

In the spring, about three-quarters of the way through the school year, the day after I upgraded my iPhone to the newest version (and, I have to say, fell in love with it again), Siobhan and I sat on her bed, about two feet apart, and spoke to each other using Facetime – with me on my device and her on her device. Mostly we spoke about how silly and redundant it was to speak through technology when it would be much simpler to just look at each other face-to-face and communicate that way. But it was fun and playful to use technology when it was so extravagantly unnecessary.

"ENOUGH!"

enough with the iPhone

it doesn't love you back (there's no app for that)

A fridge magnet that Siobhan bought for me during her Grade 10 Latin studies.

I then went next door to my room, which shares a wall with Siobhan's room. I realized that I had forgotten to ask her a question, so I phoned her: my iPhone to her cellphone. (I kept my voice down for the first question so she wouldn't hear me through the wall.)

"Hello."

"Hello. Is Siobhan there?"

"Yes." (Her voice – flat, emotionless – proves that she is not sure who's calling her.)

"It's me!"

"Dad!" (Her voice now a tad indignant.)

"How come your voice drops, how come there's no excitement, when you know it's me?"

"I don't know, Dad ... Why are you calling me?"

"Well, I have a question."

"Ahhh ... why not just come next door and ask me in person?"

"This is easier."

"Oh."

"Are you taking Latin again next year? If the answer is 'yes', knock on the wall once. If the answer is 'no', knock on the wall twice."

"What? Why don't I just tell you over the phone ... since we're already on the phone!? We are talking on the phone, you know, Dad ..."

"I know. But this is more fun. It's the old-fashioned way to communicate. You know, like smoke signals, or banging on tree trunks, or yodeling across alpine valleys."

"... OK ..."

"So, are you taking Latin next year?"

"Well, I think so. I've asked Mr. Skinner a few times and he says he thinks so."

"You're not sure?"

"No. But I assume I am taking it."

"OK. So knock on the wall once, so that I know your answer is 'yes'."

(Siobhan knocks twice on the wall.)

"Huh?! You just knocked twice."

"Oops, sorry, I should have only knocked once!"

"OK, so this time knock just once."

(Siobhan knocks once on the wall.)

"There."

"Oh, so you're taking Latin next year. Great."

"Yes, I think so. I'm pretty sure I am."

"OK. Thanks for the information. See you soon. Love you. Bye."

"Love you. Bye."

"Siobhannie. One more thing. I'll be in my room. If you want me, you can bang on the wall, or phone me, or text me, or send me an email. Or just come on over and visit me in person!"

"Dad!"

Of course Siobhan knows no other world than one which is wholly and intricately wired. Earlier I mentioned that humans ("homo sapiens" or "wise man") have been known as "homo ludens" or "people at play," but we could just as easily be known as "homo technologicus" or "technological beings." One day when she was six years old I came upon Siobhan quite intently occupied with something on the computer screen. I asked her what she was doing and she said that she was learning to type. She had discovered on her own a site put up by the BBC called "Dance Mat Typing," which has a goat dressed in a purple outfit and the phrase "Come type with me!" on the homepage.

Kids are led through 12 stages, and as they type letters correctly they are met with a celebratory bugle-blast or a "Way to go!" and when they type letters incorrectly they are met with a corrective "Type on me!" or a few descending musical notes. Before long, Siobhan was slowly touch-typing, assisted the whole way by a purple goat speaking in what I think of as a Liverpudlian accent.

I recently popped on to the Dance Mat Typing site and despite being met with such encouraging phrases as "Houston, we have lift-off!" and "Groovy!" and "Rock'n'roll!" I simply do not have the patience, now, to learn how to touch-type. So here I am, a person who has spent his whole life typing (I've used an IBM Selectric; I bought my own portable Brother typewriter just before my freshman year at Notre Dame; my first work-related IBM computer used 500 KB Double-Sided Single-Density 8-inch floppy disks; and then on through a whole assortment of desktops, laptops and hand-helds) and my daughter is the touch-typer ... and I am not. And what is particularly dispiriting (if I let it be so) is that she discovered the BBC site on her own, and then taught herself, and had fun doing it.

Yet it is important to realize, despite the virtual and real wires that crisscross our planet and the heavens, and that enable six-year-olds to teach themselves some pretty sophisticated activities, that one-fifth of the world lives without electricity, the technology that capacitates all the others. One-fifth! That's about 1.3 billion people, give or take. We're not just talking about access to electric power sources for computers and TVs and the most recent version of "Call of Duty." We're talking about access to electric light and electric refrigeration – something that every single person in the West could not survive without. (I know I certainly could not.) And according to *The Economist,* the number of people without electricity will "tick up to 1.5 billion by 2030" as "population growth outstrips electrification."

We sometimes look back on Roman times – the early monarchy, through the republic and on through the empire – and recall dismissively that there were huge economic disparities between the rich and the poor, with the superwealthy dining on flamingo tongues and pheasant brains while most got by on corn and cabbages, but let's not forget the huge economic disparities of our own time. There are, to state the obvious, people in our age who quaff thousand-dollar bottles of wine, while others – including the one in eight people worldwide who do not have access to safe drinking water – have to travel hours to fill up a plastic jug of water for essential use.

Every kid, Siobhan included, takes the things and the technology they have around them for granted. As young children we believe, or somehow come to intuit, that we are not unusual, that others must have similar lives: "I love Count Chocula, everyone loves Count Chocula!"; "Look what I got for Christmas, what did you get?" Only when we start to go to school – or start to expand our worldview outside of our own home-life and see others markedly different from us – do we start to realize that others are not like us.

I have to admit that I was even slower. Not until the third year of my BA, spent in Ireland studying Joyce, Yeats and Beckett, did I realize that there were non-Catholics. As I mentioned earlier, I attended nothing but Catholic schools up until the age of about 21. I guess I knew that there were people who were not Catholic, and perhaps I had even spoken to a few, but that was far from truly appreciating the vast religious, geographic and intellectual richness and otherness of the world. People who were non-Catholics – interesting and curious and distinct people who were non-Catholics? Really? Before I spent a year in Ireland (itself an overwhelmingly Catholic

THE WORLD'S FIRST COMPUTER, C. 100 BCE

This may not look like much, but the Antikythera mechanism has been called the world's first analog computer.

Built around the 1st century BCE, its elaborate system of 30 interlocking bronze gears were used to calculate the positions of the sun and moon, as well as other astronomical phenomena, including the phases of the moon, eclipses, and perhaps even the locations of other planets. Below is a contemporary reconstruction by Mogi Vicentini of what the mechanism may have looked like.

In *The Republic*, Cicero also spoke about a "globe" and another "ancient invention" that were capable of displaying the movements of the sun and moon and planets.

country) I had simply never given the idea much thought.

These days, technology enables, instantaneously, Siobhan and her friends to see that there are differences everywhere. Siobhan, in the midst of her game-playing and music-listening and photo-sharing, also knows that there are kids worldwide that do not have clean drinking water, and that there are a range of sexual orientations, that there are heart-wrenching events in her neighbourhood and in the Philippines, as well as opportunities for her to make a positive impact. She can and does travel – imaginatively, creatively, intellectually – just by using the glittering screens that are in front of her.

WE'LL ALWAYS FIND A WAY

Of course technology can be used for nefarious purposes now, but people always find ways to do what they want to do. In *The Annals*, written around 117 CE, Tacitus talks about how, during Nero's time, Rome imported its degeneracy: "The result was that anything capable of being corrupted or of causing a corruption was on view in the city, and young people were becoming decadent through fads from overseas – visiting the gymnasia, loafing around, and indulging in degrading love affairs."

In our apartment Siobhan and I share the same computer – an IBM ThinkPad that is not particularly beautiful and not particularly fast, but does, for now, work just fine. Every once in a while we both "need" to get on the machine at the same time – me to check my email and her to do homework; or me to do work and her to check her email – but for the most part we manage to share the old beast fairly well. Of course we both leave scattered notes and scraps of paper around. Once she left a couple of sticky notes lying next to the laptop:

"Let's see. I feel sexy. What has come over me … Here it comes again."
"It's beyond me. Help me mommy. I'll be good, you'll see. Take this dream away. What's this?"

I was initially a bit concerned about these thought scraps, these small yellow pieces of paper that seemed to be speaking of teenage angst and inner torment that Siobhan may have been trying to tell me about in the most direct way she knew how. When I finally asked Siobhan about them, a couple days later, she laughed a knowing and teasing laugh: "Oh yeah, those are lines from *The Rocky Horror Show*. Remember I was in our high school production last year? I thought you'd like those little quotes next to your computer. Ha! Kinda worried were you!?"

VOCABULARY CHECKLIST

communication – n. communicatio
free – adj. liber
teach – v. doceo
technical – adj. artificialis
tool – n. instrumentum

PRACTICING THE LANGUAGE

We all use technology and we always will.
Utimur omnes novis artibus, et semper utemur.

How we communicate and perhaps even how much we communicate – using everything from real and virtual word-scraps to long and contemplative epistles – changes over time. Some letters that Seneca or Pliny the Younger wrote, on wax-coated wooden tablets that were then hinged together by leather straps, went on for pages and with the writer, it seems, always having an eye on a future and expanded audience, and often on some form of permanent posterity. One of Seneca's letters, 90, goes on for about 5,000 words in its English translation and talks at length about the various technologies of his and preceding ages, including the loom, the saw, hypocasts (under-floor heating), millstones, weapons of war, apartment buildings that soar "storey upon storey," and a form of early, fragrant air conditioning that saw saffron-infused water vapour sprayed from a "great height from hidden pipes" upon dinner guests.

In contrast, some of my letters (or, more accurately, emails and text messages) to Siobhan consist of precisely one letter – a "K," itself a shortened version of "OK"; or a "D" just to remind her that I am her Dad; or sometimes the emotional and affectionate "L." And when I am feeling particularly affectionate toward her I sometimes elaborate by sending her the infinitely more intense message "LLLLLLLLL." There is no elegance to these communications, and for that I blame this intuitive technology in which we all swim so effortlessly. What I lose of the philosophic and multivalent eloquence of Seneca, I make up for (so my sad internal logic goes) with frequency and repetition.

COLD, HARD TALENTS

A Vestal Virgin from Roman times. Here is someone who I think does her job well. She dresses demurely, looks rather stern and uninviting, is cast in harsh shadow, and seems about as warm as a block of stone.

Humour can also be an important way to keep some sense of sanity around the swirling, ever-changing world of technology. In the fall, not long after Siobhan started Grade 10, she and I went in search of a new cellphone and related contract to replace her out-of-date phone and lapsed contract. Over several weeks we investigated a wide assortment of phones and plans, and then, after some wondering and weighing of options, she decided on a three-year contract with Virgin Mobile for an attractive cellphone with a full qwerty keyboard. As she said: "A lot of my friends have that same phone,

Dad. I think it's a good one." As we left the store I expressed my enthusiasm for the choice of phone that she had made, and the fact that a carefully considered decision had finally been reached. I also reminded her that the phone came with a "three-year virgin contract" and that I expected her, as she moved through the next three years of her middle teens, to abide by the contract! This sort of "Dad humour" may not be thought of as tremendously amusing to teenaged girls, but I have found that it sometimes works for me.

Technology is, after all, a metaphor for what humans do and think about. I'm not sure it is any more or less complicated than that. Technology leads to good and bad things: to creativity and destruction, to productivity and insignificance. It leads to prisons that we choose to live inside (to use Hannah Arendt's phrase) and it leads to those benefits that we find on the altar of freedom (to use Abraham Lincoln's phrase). I think Siobhan appreciates both sides of that story. And if she chooses to seek out more information on these various prisons and freedoms, she's likely to follow her investigations in her own way and at her own speed, using whatever screen and keyboard is close at hand.

SEEKING THE AVAILABLE TECHNOLOGY

As a way to aid my Latin and Roman cultural studies, I started following various tweets, including @latinlanguage, @LatinProgramme and @Elder_Pliny. I'm not a conspiracy theorist and I'm not particularly suspicious, but I did notice that the first tweet I received after signing up for @latinvocab was the following, which seemed to invoke and encourage me directly by name:

peto, petere, petivi, petitus => make for, seek, beg/ask for

CHAPTER NINE

CLEOPATRA AT THE BREAKFAST TABLE

"For he believed that any time not devoted to study was wasted."
Pliny the Younger, *Letters*

"If only parents would not rush them through their studies!"
Petronius, *The Satyricon*

AT THE BREAKFAST TABLE and at the dinner table Siobhan and I talk about anything and everything. Sometimes we share whatever passing snippet of inconsequential information has recently happened upon us (a silly joke we've heard, a local politician's facile opinion or facetious blabber spurting from the radio or the TV, or a reference to a story spoken by a friend).

On weekday mornings before her school day starts, when she is not fully awake, I may try to sneak in a more elaborate or illustrative story, or even (in my attempt to pass on some paternalistic insight) a tale that has some lesson or moral to it. I'm never sure if she gets the full context or relevance, but that doesn't bother me – perhaps it settles into her imagination over the course of the day or at some point or place in the gossamer of the distant future.

CLEOPATRA – ALWAYS PEARLY AND ALWAYS FASCINATING

Many painters have produced work based on Pliny's pearl story. Here are four (clockwise from top left): William Kent, 1685–1748, "Cleopatra dropping the pearl into the wine"; Gerard Hoet, 1648–1733, "The Banquet of Cleopatra" (detail); Giambattista Tiepolo, 1696–1770, "The Banquet of Cleopatra" (detail); Jacob Jordaens, 1593–1678, "Cleopatra's Feast" (detail).

One morning I thought she might be entertained by the famous story of Cleopatra and the pearl. According to Pliny the Elder, and retold often by many others, Cleopatra bet her lover at the time, Mark Antony, that she could spend 10 million sesterces on one banquet (maybe $5 million in our money, give or take). Just imagine Cleopatra, widely known as one of the most beautiful, wanton and manipulative of women, teasing with such ostentation one of the most powerful men of the Roman world.

As the story or legend goes, after the first course of their lavish feast had been consumed, a servant placed before Cleopatra a vessel containing vinegar. Cleopatra, "headstrong" and "haughty" as Pliny calls her, took one of her earrings off, dropped the pearl in the vinegar, waited for it to dissolve and then drank. According to Pliny, the pearl was no ordinary pearl – it was the "largest of all time."

Even though many historians have doubted this pearl-as-victuals event actually happened (and there is some speculation that Cleopatra merely swallowed the undissolved pearl whole, and "subsequently recovered it in the natural course of events" as translator John Healy speculates), it still is a remarkable story of decadence, seduction and power. And I'm sure that it impressed Mark Antony, even though he was by this time already completely and utterly smitten by Cleopatra, as Julius Caesar had been earlier.

Sometimes during a meal, Siobhan tells me her own food stories. Once she told me about food fights that regularly take place among the boisterous lunch tables at her school.

"Nearly every day at school, Dad, there's a food fight."

"What? Really?"

"Yep."

"Where are the teachers?"

"Well, sometimes they just step out for a moment. And then they come back just when the fight is over."

"Really?"

"Oh, yeah. The fights are funny. We're all laughing at our table. At first the Grade 9 students would get scared when they saw a food fight and run out of the caf. And the Grade 10 boys are standing up laughing and having a great time – they love it. And the Grade 11 students are like, 'Come on you guys, grow up'! And the Grade 12 students, the girls, they just kind of watch it all."

"Yikes."

"Once I got hit on the head with something but I didn't really know what it was. And it didn't really hurt."

"What about the people who work in the kitchen? Don't they do anything?"

"They don't really see what's going on. Although they must hear some of what's going on. Like when an orange flies across the room, maybe 30 feet, and hits someone."

At other times the conversation at the table is not much more than a few grunts, try as I might to draw her out and encourage stories about the things that she considers important or worthy. Here is an example of what can seem like the morning's entire conversation:

"Siobhanny, why don't you put some jam on your toast?"

"I'm too lazy."

"You're too lazy to put jam on your toast?"

"Yep."

"OK."

At other times of the day there is a torrent, a riverrunning gurgle of words from Siobhan:

"Dad, listen to this song I'm working on. I don't have all the chords figured out, but it's pretty close."

"Can you make me a cup of tea? Please?"

"I got a 98 on my music theory exam. Thanks for helping me study, Dad."

"Come and look at these new earrings I just made. I used some Japanese paper, and some beads, and then I just kind of designed the dangly parts."

THE STAFF (AND CARBON) OF LIFE

A loaf of bread, baked in Pompeii on August 24, 79 CE.

"I'm making myself a cup of tea. Want one?"

"What do you think about this sweater? What do you think about this shirt? Now that I cut the sleeves off, I really like it. What do you think?"

Sometimes Siobhan and I weave together a remembered story that we were both part of, with each of us adding certain details to shape and enliven the full story. One story we like to retell involves our walking through the small zoo in High Park that I mentioned earlier – the park that Ernest Hemingway was so fond of. Siobhan was six years old and we had gone there late one evening, just as the park was about to close. As we were walking around, looking at the bison and the yaks, unknown to us the park authorities locked up the eight-foot fence that led out of the park, and so in order to get out of the zoo we had to climb over the fence. There was a speck of the "outlaw," of the "let's hope we don't get caught," in scaling the fence and dropping to the other side. But we made it out of the zoo just fine, no police were involved, and the adventure has given us a shared narrative that we can recapture whenever we want to.

One story that we like to relate to others, including her friends, is the time when I was giving her a driving lesson and we were confronted by the police. Neither Siobhan's mother nor her grandmother drive and I am convinced that she should learn how to drive and feel comfortable behind the wheel. Since she has been about ten, I have taken her for driving lessons. This particular lesson (she was 11 years old at the time), I thought we should head to the large open parking lot of a local grocery store, which I knew would be empty on a Sunday afternoon. She was not tall enough to both steer and operate the pedals (that came later, when she was about 14) so she sat in my lap as we drove around, with her hands on the steering wheel and my feet controlling the accelerator and the brake. We went back and forth a few times, and did a few loose, looping arcs around the parking lot, and then came to a stop. Suddenly, a police car raced into view and stopped beside us on the passenger's side, facing in the opposite direction. Siobhan immediately popped into the passenger's seat. The police car had come to rest so close to ours that there was no way the passenger door could be opened.

The officer rolled down his window, and then tapped on our passenger window, making a motion to roll it down.

"What are you doing?" he asked.

I started to respond that I was just taking my daughter out for a driving lesson …

"I'm not asking you," came the sharp response. "I'm asking her."

"Oh, my Dad and me are just going for a drive," said Siobhan a bit nervously.

At that point the officer allowed me to speak, so I explained what we were doing, how her mother and grandmother didn't drive, that I wanted to make sure that she knew how to drive, blah blah blah. Fortunately he did not ask Siobhan's age, because it would have been a bit embarrassing telling him that she was fully five years younger than she should have been for the first of such lessons.

We got off with an informal warning. I think the officer, seeing us from afar and fearing that some nefarious activity was underway, was pleased to see the harmlessness of the situation. And Siobhan and I were left with a good story that we can share with others.

THE STORY OF FOOD

A mosaic from a second-century CE villa at Tor Marancia, Italy, tells the story of food and upcoming mealtimes.

It's probably not such a great idea to allow your kid to drive when she is still years away from legally being allowed to do so, but this interaction with the police didn't slow us down. We continued our driving lessons – sometimes on graveled country roads, or at nighttime in High Park, or through the snow so that she can get used to what that feels like – and Siobhan has done much more pre-16 driving than any of her friends, something that I think will lessen the stress when it comes to getting her first driver's licence.

Sometimes over mealtime I get a bit excited about something that I've just read, and if I can convince her to listen, I may read a chunk from a book at the ready. "Scoopenzie, listen to this," I segue from whatever we were talking about toward what I want to talk about. "I often think that parents are much more worried about their kids now than they have ever been, and then I read this," and I'll launch into a bit of Plautus, from the play *A Three-Dollar Day*:

> Regard for your father is what I should expect … I hope you
> never get into bad company … I hope you never exchange a
> single word with any undesirable person … I know what people
> are like these days; I know what things are coming to. … I know
> 'em – destructive, avaricious, malicious people who treat sacred
> things as profane, public property as their own private property
> … Oh, it makes me weep to think that I should have lived to see
> such a generation … I'll thank you never to have anything to do
> with such manners nor form your character after that pattern.
> Stick to the good old ways … and do as I tell you. I hate to see …
> the filthy perverted manners that pass for morality nowadays.

"See," I may chide her. "Parents 2,000 years ago were just as worried about their kids as we are today. That's a good thing to know – especially for me to know. And by the way, don't develop any filthy perverted manners!"

With random books and music CDs scattered about on our dining table and on most available surfaces of the apartment, there are a lot of conversation threads just waiting to be picked up and sewn into the rest of our talk: anecdotes about Blind Willie Johnson, Buckminster Fuller, Werner Heisenberg, Emily Dickinson, Apsley Cherry-Garrard and a host of other interesting people that I talk about and that I tell her she will hear more about when she heads off to university. Kids need to know (as I said, there might be a "moral" to some of the stories I tell) that the world is bursting with diverse and curious opinions, that knowledge of science and art and history are essential for any thinking person to have a sense of context and points of comparison. I've often said to her that there is not just one way to see and explain the world – that there are a multitude of ways to interpret the everyday mysteries and the ephemeral facts that we see every day around us. And I don't hide the fact that I get very worried when I hear a religion or a person say that they know the correct and true answers: that they know the right way to think and to do and to act.

Often Siobhan and I will talk about things that she knows much more about than I do.

"Tom Waits, Dad, you have to admit his early stuff is really great."

"Umm. I couldn't really say."

"Oh yeah, his first two albums are love songs. Very melodic. I listen to them all the time. It's only with his later stuff that he gets all gravelly and mumbly and grumbly."

"Well, can you play a few songs for me so I get what you mean?"

"Sure."

One time there was an item on the radio about girls being harassed on public transit while wearing their school uniforms. Apparently some man had been leering at the girls, and they had felt threatened. After the girls reported it to their teachers, the police and the news media got involved. As the radio story played itself out, Siobhan noted a part of the picture was not being discussed by any of the parties interviewed. She did not think the uniform really had anything to do with the story. "This sort of stuff happens all the time, Dad." She wasn't saying that the threatening behaviour was not to be taken seriously, and she certainly was not blaming the victims. But she did state, quite objectively, that this sort of behaviour happens frequently, that she had witnessed it, and that people, especially girls her age, need to be protective but not overly frightened or put off by this sort of behaviour. For her, the item on the news had a direct and familiar connection. She was able to discuss it with objectivity and local wisdom, assessing each opinion that came to us through the radio, and then arrive at her own observations and conclusions. "Why are they pointing out the school uniforms, when the problem really has nothing to do with that? It's a much bigger deal."

Sometimes our conversations have a certain mundane charm.

"Dad, look. Do I have a double chin?"

"No, Siobhanny, of course you don't!"

"But one of my friends says that I do. Look from the side. There, see what I mean? But I think I've come to the conclusion that I don't."

"Good."

"But when I whistle ... look ... I have a double chin when I whistle. And I like to whistle."

"Sio-Sio, when people whistle, they get a double chin – you have to, in order to expel the air. Look, see, I have a double chin when I whistle too."

"Yes, but you're 54. Sorry. But you are older and so your skin isn't as tight. Look when I whistle. See, I think I have a double chin!"

"Oh, thanks, so I'm an old fart."

"No, seriously, Dad, look. Do I have a double chin?"

ROMAN WORDPLAY

We sometimes think that English is the main font of wordplay, but the Romans also had similar fun. Here are a couple of examples:

Latin palindrome (a sentence that reads the same backwards as forwards) "In girumimus nocte et consumimur igni" ("We enter the circle after dark and are consumed by fire"), which was used to describe the action of moths.

Latin anagram (scrambling letters of one phrase to form another) "Quid est veritas?" ("What is truth?") mes "Est vir qui ad est." ("It is this man here.")

In a forthcoming chapter I talk about my idea of hell: it could be defined as one child and two parents at the mealtime table: the parents intently pursuing the child: the parents inspecting and investigating the child: the parents lasering in on the child with mundane or intrusive questions. But the benefit of not having a rambunctious tumult of kids at meal times (as I had when I was a kid) is that it's not all yelling and arguing and noise. When it is just Siobhan and me at the table, we can talk about any number of things simultaneously. She can tell me about a boy in one of her classes who told her about having been kicked out of school and how he had to go to court that day, without somehow letting his parents know. About a new song she is learning on the guitar, that she had heard wandering around the Internet and that now she's trying to learn to play for an upcoming student coffeehouse. Or about a girl who recently got into a screaming match with her friends over some stupid thing that another student may or may not have said.

I too talk about a range of strange or quotidian things. About how I was reading that if we were able to take every bit of space out of every atom in our bodies, and leave just the protons, neutrons and electrons, the entire population of the world – all seven billion of us – could fit in a space about the size of a normal chicken egg. About how I found four picture frames downstairs that must have been left by someone moving out of the building, and how I can now frame four more family photographs for our wall. Or about how, like Heisenberg, I constantly wonder about how we change things by looking at them: how by merely observing things, we actually change their movement and their position, and how that leads to all sorts of uncertainties. And so we wander back and forth randomly among these sorts of delicious meanderings.

And just how does a father talk to his inquisitive teenaged daughter about sex and drinking and drug abuse and boys and all of the other hazards (to call them "topics" or "issues" does not begin to acknowledge most parental fears) that I know are lurking, lasciviously and invitingly, just around the next corner? How does a father broach these topics in a way that is informative or beneficial, that does not push her away or shut her down, and that may even provide some actionable guideposts that she can make use of?

I have no idea.

When she brought home her yearbook from Grade 9, I must have spoken with some fondness about my high school yearbook, which she of course then immediately asked to see. I was initially resistant, remembering that there were all sorts of stupid, sexual and immature comments and drawings scattered throughout it, courtesy of my schoolmates at the time, at the all-boys school I attended, Vancouver College. But she was equally insistent, so I brought the book out.

There, on page after page, were nasty, sexual, infantile and occasionally funny comments and drawings. She leafed through the book and I do not think she missed one of the embarrassing objects on show – the multitude of drawings and comments that showed so much teenaged insight and wisdom: "Hey, Pete, you are such a suckhole" and "I'll think of you when I'm taking a crap" and "I hope I never have to see your ugly face again" and other such marginalia.

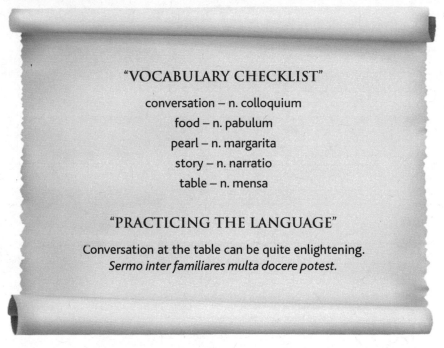

"VOCABULARY CHECKLIST"

conversation – n. colloquium
food – n. pabulum
pearl – n. margarita
story – n. narratio
table – n. mensa

"PRACTICING THE LANGUAGE"

Conversation at the table can be quite enlightening.
Sermo inter familiares multa docere potest.

Why am I relaying this little aside about my high school yearbook? I am sad to say that I thought for a few minutes afterwards (in fact, for some time afterwards) that by walking through my high school yearbook with her, I had covered at least a few items of my fatherly duty – I had managed to show her what boys can be like, I had articulated various topics of a sexual nature, and I had managed to demonstrate that we all go through silly and immature moments (or years) of self-discovery. That mere task of sharing with her these moments proved to me that I was indeed a responsible parent. I cannot say that my illustrative exhortations were on equal footing with Seneca's ("Then we must despise wealth: it is the indenture of slavery. Abandon gold and silver and whatever else is a burden to family happiness.") but it was, at the moment, the best that I could do.

One of Siobhan's major enthusiasms – a way of telling her own story to herself and to others – is decorating her room. Around her bed and the desk where she does her homework there are a series of family and friend photographs that she has hand-framed by wrapping thin strips of homemade Japanese paper around cut-out cardboard. On the corkboard above her desk there are more photographs, and the dust-jacket from the book *The Tale of Ginger & Pickles* by Beatrix Potter, and programs from various shows that she's seen on Broadway. And there are snippets of lyrics from some of her favourite songs scattered about on sticky-notes:

"This is fact not fiction for the first time in years." From "A Lack of Color" by Death Cab for Cutie

"The wind is making speeches, and the rain sounds like a round of applause." From "Time" by Tom Waits

"Oh what a perfect day, to think about myself. My feet are firmly screwed to the floor. What is there to fear from such a regular world!" From "Perfect" by The THE

"I use my blindfold to dry my tears. The stage is empty and tired of light." From "The Fan Dance" by Sam Phillips

"God is a concept by which we measure our pain." From "God" by John Lennon

On one wall she has nailed a grid of album covers that she has collected from various sources, including from her mother, from a long-time friend of mine, Mary, or that have been purchased for a dollar or so at various second-hand shops:

"The Rocky Horror Picture Show" soundtrack

The Beatles' "Second Album"

Duke Ellington and His Orchestra, "Hi-Fi Ellington Uptown"

Van Morrison, "Moondance"

Neil Young, "After the Gold Rush"

The "Stand By Me" soundtrack.

And then randomly arranged about the room are posters and small hanging lights and other things that she has made, including dangling and sprouting and affixed items made out of beads and paper and pipe cleaners and yarn. Entering the room visitors see colour and movement and personality: a boisterous mash-up of ideas and explorations and memories.

It doesn't bother me that Siobhan might think the only reason I am studying Latin (and that, I have to admit, is going exceedingly slowly) is to hang out and spend more time with her, to hear more of her developing story. It doesn't even bother me when she sometimes makes a funny or dismissive face when I want to talk about the bizarre habits of some of the Roman emperors, or when I get excited when I hear snippets of Latin on the radio or on TV, or when I say that talking about Cleopatra is more interesting and more insightful than talking about local city politics or whether Nicki Minaj has a new album coming out.

THE UNSWEPT APARTMENT

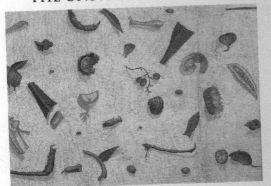

Our kitchen floor often looks the same. This mosaic, from the first century, is often referred to as "The Unswept House."

The one thing I've come to appreciate over the process of writing this book is that the most important stories – more important than a father and daughter talking about Cleopatra, Leonardo da Vinci, or Leonardo DiCaprio over breakfast, more important than families sharing stories about grandparents and grandchildren, more important even than the stories that Ovid and Shakespeare and Joyce tell us about what it means to be human – are the stories that we tell ourselves. Those unique, repetitious, internal stories that we all have and that take up such a huge part of every moment of our lives. These shifting stories – transient, histrionic, epic, prosaic, chimerical, or in the words of Sir Arthur Quiller-Couch, the "wanderings, alightings, fertilisings" of our thought – are what keeps the world spinning. Delusions. Ambitions. Memories. Prestidigitations. Rights. Wrongs. Slights. Needs. Conceits. Phantasies. Et cetera. Perhaps all these are rooted in our two great appetites (again invoking Quiller-Couch): "love and hunger." Always repeated and recreated, remembered and misremembered. As Maggie Koerth-Baker, science editor of BoingBoing.net says, an important part of our identities is "the stories we tell ourselves about ourselves."

Without these self-constructed stories, we would not have successes, failures, a past or a future. They are never crystalline (they are simply too puzzling and labyrinthine), they can never be recorded (for by recording them, they are altered), and they can never be fully understood (because they are based on arcana that can never be figured or cast). They can never even be shared (although they may seem to have the glisten of perfection in our minds, they unbuckle and dissemble when they come in contact with the volatile, external air). But they are there. I am full of them and Siobhan is full of them. And these internal stories are, in their own way, the rickety, generating foundation upon which everything else rests.

PEARLS OF WISDOM, OR NOT

Cleopatra wearing pearls: a tight pearl necklace around her neck, a dangling pearl necklace, and pearls in her hair, at the top of her forehead. One of the things I like about the image on this coin is that most people would not consider the subject to be a world-beating beauty who could conquer the hearts of the most powerful men of her age. Large nose, thin lips, small chin, flabby neck: power is in the eyes of the beholder, I guess.

CHAPTER TEN

FACEOFF, FACETIME, FACEBOOK

"Behave towards a friend as though you remembered
that he could easily become your enemy."
Publilius Syrus, *Maxims*

"… good teachers, good family, relatives, and friends …"
Marcus Aurelius, *Meditations*

I N THE ENTRANCE HALL of our small apartment there are about 80 framed photographs
haphazardly assem-
bled on the wall.
The faces and the times
and the stories are all
jumbled together.

There is a photo-
graph of Siobhan (as yet
unborn and unnamed)
still in her mother's belly.

YOUTH, AND AGE

My paternal grandmother
and grandfather in
their tintype portrait,
which I reproduced as a
photograph for our family
wall.

Of my voluminous immediate family in 1959 (my mom, dad, me, three brothers and six sisters) taken in Mamaroneck, New York, and then again in 1989, taken in Toronto, Ontario (this time sans father, who had died a few months after the earlier photograph had been taken). Of smiling Siobhan at various points of her life: wandering among the fields and cows of Ireland with her maternal relatives, and enjoying the ancient ruins of Turkey near a touristy Trojan Horse with a few of her friends. Of my paternal grandparents, who I never knew – an elegant flowering and ribboned hat perched on my grandmother's head, and a dashing waxed moustache, complementing his silk bow-tie, on my grandfather. Of my maternal grandmother and grandfather seated at the opposite edges of a 1927 family portrait (proud parentheses to their ten children arranged randomly between them). Of my brother Bob and some of his soldier buddies lounging around on a patch of dirt in Vietnam – one of the soldiers sits in front of a truck with the word D-I-E-S-E-L stenciled on it – his body blocks out the last three letters of the word – a presage of what would happen to my brother some years later. And there are various photographs of Siobhan and me, including one where she, a few days old, has fallen asleep on my chest, her chubby pink fingers loosely clutching the folds of my shirt.

The myriad faces assembled there evoke longings, repines, vagaries: mysteries approached and mysteries that were never heeded. I am aware of how many faces are missing, and how much individual and collective history will remain forever undocumented. Evolutionary scientists speculate that about 99.9 percent of all species of animals and plants that have ever existed are now extinct. Charles Darwin puts it matter-of-factly: "The number of specimens in all our museums is absolutely as nothing compared with the countless generations

EVERY PICTURE TELLS
A FEW STORIES

of countless species which certainly have existed." On our photography wall, 99.9 percent of the story of Siobhan and me is not represented, is extinct. There are no photographs of the eight step-brothers and four step-sisters I acquired when I was ten years old, none of my great-grandparents, none of most of my friends from over the years, none of the schools I attended or of my favourite writers or from various jobs that I've had. There are no photographs of many of Siobhan's friends, none of her Irish roots stretching back more than two generations, and none of her quotidian triumphs (good report cards, piano competitions won, ballet classes taken). Those small, piercing moments that at one point in time seemed to encapsulate the whole wide world (a first tooth ... a ride on a camel ... a visit from my sister who lives in Arizona ... the first day of school) are now worn smooth by other moments and have started to dissolve and fade. All of us, Siobhan and me included, live our lives blithely weetless and unencumbered by the multitude of extinctions through which we have passed and continue to pass.

Siobhan is proud of the random quirkiness of the photo wall, and when her friends come over she highlights some of her favourites and listens to her friends' comments: "Vonnie, is that you with a pink bathing suit stuck on your head?" "Is that your dad with hair!?" "Hey, that's me in the photo with Gordon Lightfoot!"

On the opposite wall from the one that gathers our friends and family, I have framed about 60 tintypes that I have bought on eBay over the years. They are small rectangles of iron, about 3 ½ x 2 ½ inches (despite their name, tintypes are sheets of iron that have been blackened by enamel or lacquer). There is a group of four women,

EVERY STORY MISSES SOME PAGES

Even Livy, author of the 142-volume history *The Dawn of the Roman Empire*, laments how much he has to leave out. Writing about the military campaigns of 197 BCE in various cities outside of Rome, he says: "A detailed report of military operations in these spots cannot really be justified when I am barely capable of providing an account of those relevant to the war fought by the Romans."

who look like sisters, dressed in full-length dresses, flowering. A young boy with a floppy silk tie and mud caked on his lace-up boots glances askance at the photographer. A young barefoot girl, her arm resting on the arm of an embroidered couch, looks out tentatively on the world. An old man and an old woman, wide-eyed, their arms interlocked, look off in the distance, perhaps winnowing through things that have disappeared or been lost over the course of their lifetime. No one is smiling, but that's because the sitters had to hold their pose for a few seconds in order to allow the photographers to work their scientific magic – suspending silver halide crystals in colloidion emulsion – and no one can hold a natural-looking smile for that long.

Siobhan and I do not know any of the names of any of the people in these tintypes. They are, to us, anonymous faces, mostly dating from the 1860s to about the 1890s. Each of the subjects had decided for one reason or another to have their faces chemically etched onto a surface of sheet iron, which they could then carry away with them to perhaps display on their mantel for everyone else to see. Every one of these tintypes is a one-off. Unlike today's technology, where an infinite number of copies can be made from the original digital image, and can be immediately emailed (manipulated and adapted, if we so desire, in any way we want) to hundreds or thousands of recipients simultaneously, tintype technology meant that there are no other copies of the images that we have on our walls. Only the original exists, only that one representation of that one moment of a person's life. It is not unlikely – especially for the older subjects – that some of the tintypes displayed on our wall are the only image that was ever taken of these specific people over the course of their life. Their elaborate lives and storied faces, the wrinkles that corduroy their foreheads, their muscled hands, the families that engendered them, the paid and unpaid work they did, the joys and sorrows of the passing days: this one small piece of iron is the only humble memory, the only surviving attempt to capture and preserve this extravagant richness.

TWO FACES, TWO BOOKS

Studying Latin and reading about the early Romans is one way to remind ourselves that the current land through which we wander is built upon exanimated people and disappearing languages. The words that we use now, to describe our friends and our families, are made up of fragments of forgotten words. The linguistic pageant that Latin has given us is not so much a terra incognita, because we did know it once, and we can still discern the sharp outlines and subtle indentations just below the surface. It is more of a terra oblivio – a land of forgetfulness – or a terra ignoratio – a land of ignorance – because we choose to forget and ignore. Civilizations and individuals continuously make decisions about what to wipe clean, what to destroy, what to erase from the collective memory. We are all involved in this ongoing act and process of extinction.

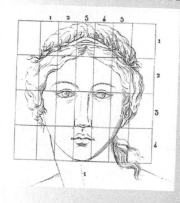

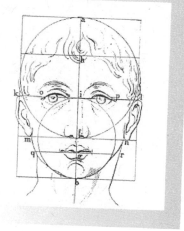

Children, by definition, work against extinction. On Facebook and the other sites that Siobhan populates, she of course has her own virtual wall of photographs and her own profile picture, which she regularly updates. Sometimes it's a picture of her playing the guitar or caught in some animated gesture. At other times it is her smile or gesture amidst a group of her smiling and gesturing friends. New photographs, new tags, new conversations, new albums, new posts, new timelines, new friends are continuously on view. All this newness seems to be saying: "I am not extinct. I am here and I am now."

VOCABULARY CHECKLIST

country – n. patria
extinction – n. exstinctio
face – n. species
individual – n. homo
share – v. communico

PRACTICING THE LANGUAGE

All people value friends and communication.
Magni facimus omnes amicorum epistolas.

Although Siobhan and I are "friends" on Facebook, I choose not to follow her very much, as some parents do their kids. I don't want to spend hours seeking out the bits of her life that I may find reason to worry about or question. Every two or three months I may pop on to take a look and a read. Mostly I see random one-way statements by Siobhan's friends as they try to be funny or silly or faux-upset:

:) hope I didn't distract you too much at work today, but I miss you SO MUCH, hope your trip was amazing, and we should get together eventually to swap stories :)

heysoo... STOP IGNORING ME OR I WILL KIDNAP YOUR CHILDREN WHO MAY OR MAY NOT ALSO BE MY CHILDREN.

siobhan when i type your name i sound it out as c o bahantehe i love your clothes

i love your smile

you are so adorable

you are the nicest person in the world that i ever met actually

how is it possible to be that nice?

i feel like sam and i are going to get you fired:D

you got to travel all over so cool!

you are an amazing singer I HEAR.. i need to hear your singing girl!

WHAAAAAAATTTTTTTTTTTTTTTTTTTT

Of course Siobhan and her friends are leaving digital footprints that are not always enveloped in wisdom or maturity, but I simply cannot get too upset about it. Sulpicia and Lucan and Petronius also left their footprints and not always was the message sage or thoughtful. Sulpicia, as we saw, had pretty typical feelings of youthful impatience and selfishness. Lucan, who wrote one of the classics of Roman literature, *Civil War*, can sometimes be overwrought, emotional and gushy: "Now come,

SIOBHAN AND FRIENDS

A recent addition to our photo wall: Siobhan (far left) and some of her friends. Knowing that each of the subjects wanted to be represented in the best possible light, I took ten photographs, and then used the best of the individual faces for this composite, digital image.

O Harmony, embracing all with eternal bond, / the salvation of nature and the muddled universe / and the sacred love of the world: now our age controls / the great decision of what is to come." And Petronius about 2,000 years ago was pretty clear that "adolescent taste is quite worthless," and grown men weren't much better. As he says: "Boys today are frivolous in school; young men are laughing-stocks in public life; and, the greatest shame of all, even when they are old they refuse to give up the mistakes they learnt earlier."

What Facebook does allow Siobhan to do is create her own community, full of people who share, or not, her interests. Being an only child – not uncommon in this age – means that she naturally looks beyond the limited structure of her own family for companionship and close confidantes. In a sense, her Facebook friends become a sort of loose, extended family. Facebook becomes a way for her to combat loneliness, to celebrate the moment, to pack and unpack some of the things that are on her mind. Facebook has well over 1 billion users because people want and need to see each other's face, to read each other's book.

And we all want to leave an imprint – whether it's a large and permanent footprint left in hardening concrete that will be seen by others that we'll never know, or whether it is a sympathetic fingerprint that is meant for one of our closest friends to help them through a trying time.

The major task of Facebook, one of the central businesses of our era, is to make as many friends as possible: to encourage people to make friends with each other, and to encourage people to make friends with the company itself. One of the ways it does this is by offering as many languages as it can. Facebook is currently available in over 75 languages, including Latin. On October 2, 2009, on the official Facebook blog, Elizabeth Linder brought Latin to Facebook. As she said in her posting, "Latin Becomes a Living Language on Facebook," this "venerable language" now "springs to life on Facebook." I'm not sure that much springing happened, but I note that 3,184 people "liked" (with the happy little "thumb-up" icon) this blog:

actually, they registered their like for this post by clicking on the Latinate "Mihi placet" icon.

Linder made sure that she noted her own background in Latin and her own affection for the language:

> Though Latin has been long out of use, for some of us, it never loses its intrigue. As a native English speaker, I enrolled in Latin to supplement my study of Romance languages. I still remember reading a translated copy of "Winnie the Pooh" in Latin, and gradually working my way through state speeches and philosophic commentary dating from the Roman Empire. When I joined Facebook a year ago, I chose a Latin phrase, "dictum meum pactum" ("my word is my bond"), as the phrase that currently appears on my Facebook business card.

I find some comfort in this digital, multinational corporation making a commitment to Latin. Perhaps it is because Facebook founder Mark Zuckerberg studied Latin. He is known to quote Latin in staff meetings and it is said that his personal motto is *Forsan et haec olim meminisse iuvabit*, which can be loosely translated as: "Maybe one of these days we will look back on all this shit and have a good laugh."

Currently Linder is working in the area of Politics and Government for Facebook. In a recent interview on YouTube, Linder spoke about how Facebook is assisting "diplomatic relations around the world" through its enabling of communication and conversations. As she said, speaking at a NATO-sponsored conference, "social media … and Facebook have become an instrument and a key player in achieving diplomatic relations" among the nations of the "global village."

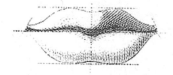

So Facebook, that great friendship encourager, has its role to play in our era not only on a person-to-person basis (as has been documented in *Connected: The Surprising Power of Our Social Networks and How They Shape Our Lives* and elsewhere) but increasingly on the international stage. There are many recent examples of social media having such internationally important roles and interventions. Perhaps most notable are the actions of Wael Ghonim, the Head of Marketing for Google's Middle East and North Africa office, who was the administrator of a Facebook page which helped spark the Egyptian uprising of 2011 and the so-called Arab Spring.

Maybe the digital footprint that Siobhan is creating – which may very well be shared with many people she'll never know, now and in the future – is just another transient moment heading, as all such moments do, toward extinction. For now it is a way for her to note and share the times of her life, the ticks of the clock and the steps of her path, and that seems like a good activity for anyone of her age.

The new friends that she gathers as she travels, when she heads off to university, and then later through her work life and beyond (as well as the friends that she leaves behind, or that leave her behind) will make up the larger arc of her life.

In earlier eras, people had the moments of their life passed along in conversations, or perhaps recorded on papyrus, and sometimes left on granite or marble or a thin sheet of iron. For Siobhan, many of the moments of her life will be left in the ethereal world of electrons and on a flickering, evanescent screen. One way or another, a lot of these stories will get worn away by the sands, winds, waters and flames of time. But for the moment, she is fighting – quite valiantly and enthusiastically I'd say – against this inevitable extinction.

CHAPTER ELEVEN

TIME IS ON MY SIDE

"The obligation to ensure that our children find pleasure ...
bids us to become children again."
Symmachus, *Letters*

"I shall find time ... I shall find time."
William Shakespeare, *Julius Caesar*

KIDS TEACH US ABOUT TIME. Or at least how time, whether we want it to or not, lurches, unstoppably, incontrovertibly, forward. As we watch those bundles of fledgling enthusiasm and investigation get older, probing and plotting the landscape as they go, we realize that we too must be getting older.

Three people whom I spent some time with and thought a lot about over the past year, and who I mentioned earlier in these pages, are no longer fledgling. Latin scholar Elaine Fantham is in her late 70s, structural engineer Morden Yolles is in his late 80s, and economist and businessman Bill Krehm just turned 100. If the youthful Siobhan has kept me aware of my gathering age, I am convinced that these three energetic elders have helped keep me young. Each of them has a strong, driving sense of exultation that borders on impatience. Each of them has a rich personal history and a desire to continue exploring and raging, in their own way, against the inevitable dying of the light.

Elaine has trouble walking and breathing, but she continues to churn out books, translations and introductions for Oxford World's Classics and other publishers, most recently on Roman literary culture, and on Seneca, Virgil and Petrarch. And with her rich sense of history and her feisty opinions, she is a great person to go to the movies with.

Mordy can be a bit rickety on his feet, but he goes to the gym every day for what he calls his visits to the shvitzeria, takes and exhibits photographs, continues to run Scaramouche, one of the finest restaurants in North America, and remains fascinated by how the Romans brought water over vast distances through the use of aqueducts, by the concrete they used to build the Pantheon, and their other engineering marvels.

Bill seems to be always cold and he often wears a hat and scarf indoors, but he plays the piano almost every day for two hours, turns out a 20-page newsletter every six weeks on economic policy and whatever else suits his intellectual fancy, still travels extensively (most recently, at the age of 99, to Venezuela, Greece and Barcelona), and recently launched a major legal case related to the federal government's fiscal policy. Bill is also pleased to relate how he dined with George Orwell in Barcelona during the Spanish Civil War, and stood guard over the corpse of Leon Trotsky in Mexico City, in August 1940.

These three surely realize that their time is winding down and yet none of them cares to talk about it. They are much too concerned about what comes next: what book to read next, what adventures their children or grandchildren are up to, what the upcoming opera season holds.

When I was in Grade 10 our main history textbook was called *The Ancient and Medieval World*. Although I don't remember doing so,

I must have stolen a copy of the book, or simply failed to return my copy as the school year ended, because I still have the book on my bookshelves. Inside its pages is a yellowing, fading sheet of mimeographed paper that includes a class assignment of 44 questions. Among the questions:

"According to legend, who founded the city of Rome?"
"What was the extent of the Roman Empire on the death of Augustus Caesar?"
"Why was the Christian Church so important after the collapse of Rome?"

I'm not sure when I was in Grade 10 that I read the introduction with any great sense of commitment or attention, but the words now take on a certain resonance. The authors, addressing the high school audience of the book, tried to invoke our confluence with the past. We students live in a land, the authors tell us, that

is the inheritor of all the knowledge and all the civilization and culture of all the nations that have existed. And you ... in this twentieth century are the heir of all the thoughts and all the acts of the men and the women who inhabited this earth before you. ... You, like Ulysses, are a part of all the experience of all mankind.

CROSSING THE RUBICON

Julius Caesar crossing the Rubicon, from my Grade 10 textbook *The Ancient and Medieval World*. When I was in my late 20s I was the founding editor of a literary and art journal that I named *Rubicon*, perhaps influenced by this dramatic drawing.

The cave-dweller of the Old Stone Age, the Egyptian driving his chariot by the Nile, the Greek mathematician, and the Roman legionary fighting for his empire in distant lands, have all contributed in one way or another to your life as you live it today.

This inclusive and encouraging statement is becoming more evident to me now, but how many teenagers – indeed, how many adults – appreciate or even have the inclination to appreciate how closely we are tied to the past?

Is there a time when we stop looking toward the future and begin to look toward the past? Perhaps this shift in attention begins in our twenties (when responsibilities begin to mount up) or when we have children (and experience the accumulating past of the young people that we watch so closely) or when we realize that we have fewer days ahead of us than we have behind us (half-way to our allotted three-score-and-ten, or at 40 years of age, 45 years of age, or can we push this thought out of our mind until we are in our 50s?). Perhaps this shift in concern away from the future and toward the past is a slowly expanding idea that begins, without words, at our first moments of consciousness and continues on over the decades until we are no longer in command of our minds and imaginations. Perhaps – as I imagine Elaine and Mordy and Bill must do – we encircle the past, present and future into one, and slowly begin to realize that these three times are each contained within the other.

WHEN?

"You mean now?" – Yogi Berra, when he was asked what time it was.

For Siobhan now, and perhaps for me when I was a teenager reading the stories within *The Ancient and Medieval World* – Hannibal and his elephants crossing the Alps, Julius Caesar crossing the Rubicon, the Visigoths and the Huns and the Vandals crossing rivers and mountains and seas to plunder Rome – there is no time but the present. High school and its multifarious pressures can be all-consuming and can quite easily blot out thoughts of the past or speculations about the future. High school is a time for the here and now. I remember in my teens complaining to my mom about some small thing or other (clothes, food, family arguments) and her saying to me: "What difference will it make ten years from now?" She was right, of course, but I'm not sure that my displeasure or concern, at that very moment, was placated.

Siobhan sometimes leaves the house complaining, it seems, about everything:

> Dad, my hair is a mess. It just hangs there. It's not wavy and it's not straight. Look at it! And I've got pimples everywhere! Look at this huge one on my chin. Hello! It's like it can talk! It's so big it looks like an eyeball! And this is the second day in a row I've worn these pants. I've got a test today in Geography. And my hair. Do you think it looks better if I twirl it, like this? Oh well, I guess I'll just put on my 50-pound backpack now and head to school. Hello pimple! Dad, where's my lunch? Did you make my lunch? Bye!

How is it possible to even begin to respond to these multiple, monumental tribulations? When she was younger and she had some passing worry I'd always say to her "Siobhan, just remember that you are the smartest and most beautiful girl in the whole wide world." But these days those words just don't have the same force. I still believe them, of course, but for Siobhan they have a certain isn't-my-dad-quaint or oh-he's-trying-to-be-nice flavour about them. These days I can't do much more than simply listen to the litany of earth-shaking stresses, and make sure that she has everything she needs for the day. "Sweets, do you have your lunch and your keys and your cellphone? Count them off: one, two, three. Got them all? Great. OK. Love you. Bye!"

David Hajdu, a professor of journalism at Columbia University, wrote a timely piece in *The New York Times* recently. "Forever Young? In Some

STUDENT OPINION

The New York Times has a special online blog for writers 13 and above. It posted a portion of the op-ed by David Hajdu and then – under the title "Is 14 a 'Magic Age' for Forming Cultural Tastes?" – asked for comments from teens. Here are a few excerpted responses:

I completely agree with the theory that 14 is a "Magic Age"... By sophomore year of high school, cliques are fully developed and it is very rare that someone breaks out and moves between cliques. Fourteen is the magic age for most.

— Grace

I mainly agree with this article. At 14, teens are starting to discover themselves and their own tastes, rather than just listening to what their friends are listening to. When I hit fourteen, my taste in music changed dramatically. Music became a necessity to me, rather than something to occasionally hear. ... the songs they discover at 14 will become the base for their musical likings.

— Cecilia

Although it is the teen age where it is said to be most exciting I do not believe it is the "Magic Age." When I look back to being in middle school, I realize how immature and annoying everybody was. Everyone thought they were so cool, even though it was the stupidest thing ever. ... I personally do not support the saying of it being the "magical age."

— Kasia

I think that when you are 14, you are at the peak of your childhood and what you do then defines who you will be in the future. It is a magical age because it is when you are mature enough for new things yet maintain the innocence of a young child.

— Ryan

Is 14 a magic age? Well when I was 12 and 13 I was just trying to listen to and watch whatever was cool. When I was 14 I started to try discovering myself. Many of the things I did discover are still with me today. It worked for me and several other people I know and it makes sense so I guess it might be right.

— Lazarus

Ways, Yes" discusses the importance of being 14, of how the 14th birthday is the "truly historic" one, and how being a young teen is a particularly "formative age." This is the time, says Hajdu, when you are "confronting the tyrannies of sex and adulthood, struggling to figure out what kind of adult you'd like to be, and you turn to the cultural products most important in your day as sources of cool – the capital of young life."

For Hajdu, the age of 14 had resonance for various musical icons. Bob Dylan, John Lennon, Joan Baez, Aretha Franklin, Carole King, Brian Wilson and Jimi Hendrix all were

about 14 "when rock 'n' roll was first erupting" with Elvis Presley. When Irving Berlin was appropriating the black music of his day, who was 14? The answers: Sidney Bechet, Jimmie Rodgers and Fletcher Henderson. When Rudy Vallee started singing through national radio broadcasts, who was 14? The answers: Billie Holiday and Frank Sinatra. And when the Beatles first appeared on *The Ed Sullivan Show*, who was 14? The answers: Bruce Springsteen, Stevie Wonder and Billy Joel.

Music imprints itself on the receptive 14-year-old ears of all of us, and sometimes it creates instantaneous musical icons. But not all of us benefit in equal ways. My endless listening to The Moody Blues inspired no musical talents, but it did give me some ideas larger than my own existence, cloaked in melodic and orchestral lyricism. To this day, I remember most of the words to most of their records: "Days of Future Past," "To Our Children's Children's Children," "A Question of Balance" and the rest. And I have downloaded a lot of their songs onto my iPhone.

Other thinkers have noticed this fertile plasticity among 14-year-old imaginations. Hajdu quotes Daniel Levitin, author of *This Is Your Brain on Music*: "Fourteen is a sort of magic age for the development of musical tastes ... Pubertal growth hormones make everything we're experiencing, including music, seem very important. We're just reaching a point in our cognitive development when we're developing our own tastes. And musical tastes become a badge of identity."

And of course this theory relates to things other than music. Ask any adult who their favourite sports heroes are and they more often than not tell you the names from the time when they were around 14: Pelé, Muhammad Ali, Mickey Mantle, Bobby Orr, Michael Jordan, Tiger Woods, Serena and Venus Williams: across the sports and across the years it is the people who made a great impact on our early teen imaginations that stay with us for the rest of our lives.

As for books – whether it is *Pride and Prejudice*, *The Lord of the Rings*, *Animal Farm*, *The Catcher in the Rye*, *Harry Potter* or *The Hunger Games* – these things that we read as young teens stay with us long after we have closed their covers.

VOCABULARY CHECKLIST

because – conj. quia

future – n. futura

past – n. praeteritum tempus

poetry – n. poesis

time – n. tempus

PRACTICING THE LANGUAGE

The age of fourteen is an important time in our lives.

Ad annum quartumdecimum pervenire magnum vitae discrimen est.

"Every age makes its own kind of genius," says Hajdu. "For hints of what the cultural giants of the future will be doing in their own time, we'd be well served to look in the ninth-grade lockers of today. … Whatever we'll be celebrating as the legacy of the 70-year-olds" of the future, he says, "it will surely belong to the 14-year-olds" of the present.

Perhaps what we hear and see and feel when we are 14 takes on such resonance because we are hungry for the resonance. We are beginning to free ourselves from our families, from what we are familiar with. We look to our friends and music and books and sports because these things satisfy our hunger for excitement and knowledge and new adventures. "I learn by going where I have to go" says Theodore Roethke, and at the age of 14 we start to search for where we have to go.

We also listen to music and read books because we can hear the singer or the author speaking to us, directly. Everyone who listens to music or reads books knows the feeling: "That's *me* in these lyrics." "This author is putting into words what I am thinking about." "This singer is singing about what I am feeling." Perhaps this shouldn't come as a big surprise – humans sing and write about human things, and some of this relates to each of us. But it still does surprise us. It delights and comforts us. Or at least it does so to me, and many others. Stephen Greenblatt, the author of *The Swerve: How the World Became Modern*, an invigorating non-fiction book about ideas and literary detective work surrounding the discovery of *The Nature of Things* by Lucretius, said to *The Harvard Gazette* in 2000: "I am constantly struck by the strangeness of reading works that seem addressed, personally and intimately, to me, and yet were written by people who crumbled to dust long ago."

These voices reach out from the past and communicate with us directly. We, in the future, if we are receptive, can hear them. The fact that I have one daughter, who may very well have a child or children of her own one day, who will in turn have children, et cetera, means that some hundreds or thousands of years from now there will be people who have come into existence entirely and exclusively because of decisions that Siobhan and I made, or did not make, in our lives. That these distant relatives cannot trace their lineage back to us matters not a whit, not a scantlet, and that they will never know or acknowledge our role in their existences will be of no consequence to them in the least. But the fact remains that they will have life, and may even wonder about their past unknown relatives, and may even imagine what these distant people way back in the early years of the 21st century were like, because of us.

A STORY TO TELL, BOTH THEN AND NOW

Trajan's Column, completed in 113 CE, continues to tell the epic story of the wars between the Romans and the Dacians.

Many people – mystics, artists, writers, scientists – have written about the simultaneity of the past, present and future, but none more succinctly than Einstein. Toward the end of his own life, Einstein wrote to the widow of a recently departed friend: "Now he has departed from this strange world a little ahead of me. That means nothing. People like us, who believe in physics, know that the distinction between past, present and future is only a stubbornly persistent illusion." Einstein knows, as Leonardo da Vinci, T. S. Eliot, St. John of the Cross and Charles Dickens do, that the past, present and future are inextricable. Or as James Joyce says in his circular book: "THE FUTURE PRESENTATION OF THE PAST."

Siobhan and I also know, in our own stilted and small ways, of the infinite connections among them.

I also know that chunks of this book may not mean anything to Siobhan until she gets much older. Here I am, in my mid-50s re-reading things that I first read in my early teens, and I am constantly saying to myself "oh, so that's what the author means," or I only now am able to make connections among various things that the author says, or I connect the words of the book I am currently reading with other books or other events in my life. It takes a while, it seems, for some things to sink in. I've read some poems by Tennyson and Eliot and Yeats a few hundred times, and could still read them every day for the next ten years and see something new in them each time. (We are, after all, a part of all that we have met and all that we have read.) I also vividly remember as a child hearing my maternal grandfather reciting lengthy swaths of Oliver Goldsmith's

OLIVER GOLDSMITH

My maternal grandfather's favourite poet, from an 1804 printing of a Goldsmith book that I own. I've always thought there was a bit of a family resemblance.

"The Deserted Village" – his rich and somewhat cranky voice rumbling out the rhymed words:

> In all my wanderings round this world of care,
> In all my griefs – and God has given my share –
> I still had hopes my latest hour to crown,
> Amidst these humble bowers to lay me down;
> To husband out life's taper at the close,
> And keep the flame from wasting by repose.

So, Siobhan, if at some time in the future – perhaps when you are old and grey and full of sleep – you do take down this book, and slowly read, and perhaps glimpse some new insight or affection in these pages that you had not seen before, and imagine that I'm still talking with you, that will give me a sense of pleasure and joy, both in the eternal present and across the years.

Chapter Twelve

FAMILY VALUES, FAMILY VIRTUES, FAMILY VOIDS

"Human life is swept along by blind chance."
Lucan, *Civil War*

"If we deserve it, the gods will show favour to my daughter."
Fronto, *Letters to His Friends*

B EING ONE OF 22 CHILDREN is rather different from being an only child. When I was a 14-year-old kid – free to define my own path and pursue my own interests within the rambunctious swirls and convulsions of my childhood home, erupting as it was with brothers, sisters, step-brothers, step-sisters and assorted other family members – I always imagined that hell would be sitting, as an only child, with my parents at dinner. Their eyes would be burrowing into me. They would be asking me questions, and then waiting for answers. They would be concerned about everything that I did, and everywhere I went and every friend that I had. They would be watching me, intently, at all times.

Fortunately, I did not have to endure the intense flames of that imagined prying, piercing, fixed-gaze hell. When you are the 20th of 22 kids, you can disappear, you can get away with things, you can have as much privacy as you want – because no one really cares that much about you or is inclined to spend their time watching out for you.

That is not the case with an only child. Siobhan, being one of one, and with separated parents, has to cope with a situation that is perhaps even one step beneath my imagined hell. At the breakfast table and at the dinner table she has to cope not with two sets of eyes upon her (and therefore with the opportunity to play one off the other, or at least to fade from one to the other) but one set upon her. One set of eyes: wondering: asking: questioning: looking:

"How was school today?" I ask her.
"Anything interesting at school today?" I ask her.
"How did your test go today?" I ask her.
"How are your classes going?" I ask her.
"Any news about your test from last week?" I ask her.
"When do you get your next report card?" I ask her.

Petty, mundane questions. The same questions, day after day. I often wonder how Siobhan puts up with it. Sometimes I am concerned that I may drive her crazy – or at least to sullenness, or frustration, or withdrawal – with my overbearing and laser-focused concerns and interests, however well-meaning they may be.

Margaret Atwood, writing about the crucial influence fathers have on daughters in the book *The First Man in My Life: Daughters Write About Their Fathers*, presents a large swath of possibility: "Encouraging, malignant or violent, benign and loving, maddening or boring, or simply looming large through their absence – for every daughter there is a father-shaped space that somehow must be dealt with, however well or badly it may have been filled."

I hope that within the multitude of mind-numbingly similar questions I ask my daughter – there, as we sit for breakfast or dinner, looking at each other – she is able to somehow separate out the particulars, the repetitions, the recurring tap-tap-tap of my inquisitions and just come to the conclusion that I care about her, that I want her to succeed (however she chooses to define that), and that I love her. I hope that the father-shaped space that I have put before her leaves her ample room to create and craft her own daughter-shaped space.

For most of us, being alive means thinking that things have turned out just the way they should have. Destiny equals acceptance. And acceptance equals destiny. How else is it possible to think? British soldiers,

IN THE FAMILY WAY

It is not my intent, within this book, to note every family value, family virtue and family void from the beginning of time until the appearance of my daughter, but I do want to record a few of the highlights. The lineage that follows is taken from various faultless sources, including *Irish Pedigrees or the Origin and Stem of the Irish Nation*, by John O'Hart (first edition, 1876):

Adam and Eve ⇨ Seth ⇨ Enos ⇨ Cainan ⇨ ... Enoch ⇨ Methuselah ⇨ Lamech ⇨ Noah ⇨ Japhet ⇨ Magog ⇨ Boath ⇨ Phoeniusa Farsaidh (AKA Fenius Farsa) ⇨ Niul ⇨ Gaodhal (AKA Gathelus) ⇨ Asruth ⇨ Sruth ⇨ Heber Scut ⇨ Baouman ⇨ Ogaman ⇨ Tait ⇨ Agnon ⇨ ... Febric Glas ⇨ Nenuall ⇨ Nuadhad Alladh ⇨ Arcadh ⇨ Deag ⇨ Brath ⇨ Breoghan (AKA Brigus) ⇨ Bilé ⇨ Milesius ⇨ Heber ⇨ ... Ollum ⇨ Cormac Cas ⇨ ... Brian Boroimhe (AKA Boru) ⇨ ... Moriertach O'Brien ⇨ ... Peter ⇨ Siobhan

By the way, the ancient name of O'Brien (as seen in the name Brian Boru, who was the King of Ireland from 1002 to 1014 CE) was Brian, signifying "The Author."

not unlike Caesar's soldiers who I referenced earlier, sang as they marched. And as they marched among the trenches during World War I, they used to sing "We're Here Because We're Here Because We're Here Because We're Here," to the tune of "Auld Lang Syne." It was, I imagine, part resignation, part a confrontation or refutation of death, part a sardonic joke about the inevitability of life, and part just a way to pass the

I LIKE LARGE FAMILIES

"I like large parties. They're so intimate. At small parties there isn't any privacy."
  – F. Scott Fitzgerald, *The Great Gatsby*

(Fitzgerald's working title for the book was *Trimalchio in West Egg* – alluding to the character Trimalchio in *The Satyricon* by Petronius.) I've always thought this quotation applies to large families as well – it certainly applied to mine.

time. And each of us, in our own metaphoric way, sings the same song, whether we attach words and music to the idea or not.

As I read the scattered memoirs of my grandparents (both my paternal grandmother and my maternal grandparents put memories and reminiscences to paper) I am reminded of how – over time – luck and chance have played their roles, their blind and deaf and dumb roles, in a daughter and her father studying Latin and other things together in the early years of the 21st century.

My paternal grandmother, Bridget (Doyle) O'Brien, was born in 1875 and died just before I was born in 1957. In her handwritten memoirs, Bridget talks about her parents, who had come over from Ireland in the 1860s: Michael Doyle (aged 24) from Wexford and Catherine Higgins (aged 18) from Enniscorthy. Before she starts in on her own story, Bridget recaps:

> One incident always comes to mind, before I go on. [Mother and Dad] had landed at Halifax from Liverpool and were to take another vessel to Quebec with another couple of friends – Mr. and Mrs. Luke Daly – but at the last hour Mother decided to remain another day as she had been very seasick on the long voyage over. The ship went as scheduled and got caught in a storm, was wrecked, and the following day the wreckage was blown to shore. None of the passengers were saved. Luke Daly and his wife were washed ashore, clasped in each other's arms. Mother's

intuition could always be depended on. So Dad left every important decision in her hands.

In 1959 my maternal grandparents wrote together "Reminiscences at 50th Anniversary," in which they intertwined their two stories to make one, seamless narrative. My grandmother spoke about how she had moved to Windsor, Ontario (where she eventually met my grandfather) because of a "catastrophic accident":

> My father, Edward Mooney, and his two eldest sons, William and Thomas, the hired man Dennis Burke, and his hired girl Addie Jones, were driving to the county fair at Essex Centre in a democrat wagon when they were struck by a passenger train. My two brothers and Dennis Burke were killed instantly and Addie Jones died a month afterwards. My brothers were aged 19 and 21 years. This was a mental shock from which my mother never fully recovered. The result was that, left without farm help, we sold the farm, animals and machinery and a new brick house (with a bathroom, the first in the settlement) and moved to Windsor when I was 12 years old.

Later in the same document, my grandfather, a medical doctor, talks about the birth of my mother, Laura, and her twin brother, who I knew as Uncle Fred, at the exact same time as what he called "La Grippe Español" was ravaging their community:

> On Easter Monday, April 21st, 1919, Laura and Wilfrid Laurier were born at the little village hospital. While I was there, our butcher, who lived across the street from our house and who had often sent us chicken broth when we were sick, was brought in with the Flu. He was in the room just above mine and I could hear him coughing so hard. One day I noticed the coughing had ceased and asked the nurse how Mr. Cuthbert was. "Oh he is fine." Later in the day I heard some bumping and scuffling on the stairway and

no one had to tell me what had happened. Our butcher was being carried out. A couple of days later the town's dentist met with the same fate and he also was carried out. I was ready to go home with the darling twins, each weighing a little over 3 pounds. The Flu was still prevalent, everyone wearing masks in public. No one was permitted to travel in or out of town.

STORIES UPON STORIES (UPON EXTINCTIONS)

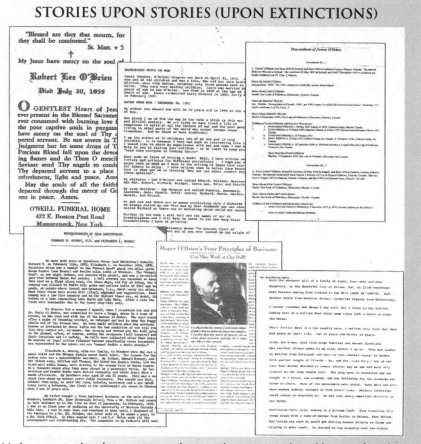

Various memoirs, documents and remembrances produced by or related to our relatives. Clockwise from upper left: prayer card produced for the death of my father; memoirs from my mother; genealogical information on the O'Briens; the autobiography of my paternal grandmother; an article on my first cousin Larry, then mayor of Ottawa, in the *Ottawa Irish Voice*; reminiscences of my maternal grandparents.

Had my paternal grandmother not been seasick after the long boat ride from Ireland, had my maternal grandmother not lost members of her family to a passing train, had my maternal grandfather not been immune from the same flu bug that carried off so many of his friends and colleagues, I would not be here and Siobhan would not be here. (And what of the families that Mr. and Mrs. Luke Daly, and that Addie Jones would have had? Their children and their travels and their capricious stories and their expanding familial legacies? Where are they? What would those people have enlivened? What would they have authorized in the decades and centuries to come?) Of course we experience only a few of fate's decrees and sentences. We do not know of the coincidences and hazards and strokes of fortune or misfortune that date from a few generations ago or a few dozen generations ago. And there is no half-life, no propagating vagaries, resulting from things that never happened.

Or even earlier still. What about the genetic mutation that gave people blue eyes and pale skin between 6,000 and 10,000 years ago – a mutation that would eventually be inherited by nearly 40 percent of Europeans, including the people that came to be called the Irish? What about the rising waters of the Hellespont 7,000 years ago, which drove farmers west, some as far as what we now know as the shores of the Atlantic Ocean? It took only a few hundred years for them to reach Spain and Ireland, as Matt Ridley so compellingly states in his fascinating discussion of how farming and trade are intimately connected.

Most of the details of our fate, of how we get to the here and now – to our own particular "tomorrow and tomorrow and tomorrow" – never get recorded. If the idea of extinction that I spoke about earlier – the 99.9 percent that does not survive – has validity, then aren't we, the ones who are still here, all of us together, the 0.1 percent?

When I was younger and imagining what sort of family I would have and how many children I wanted, I usually thought about having eight kids. Four sets of twins. I imagined – perhaps because it was the only thing I knew – the same sort of raucous house that I had when growing up. Among these imagined eight, I anticipated a few boys. Nothing too strange there – most fathers, I think, imagine that they will have a son. Things didn't quite work out as I had imagined.

One child.

A girl.

Is the world other than what it is? I guess not.

There are some advantages to not having eight kids, to being just a single father and a single daughter. Spontaneity can be one of them. And so too is being able to follow the fantastical suggestions that a daughter makes.

The summer before we started studying Latin together, Siobhan suggested a few days of summer camping. I said yes pretty quickly. I know that such opportunities are rare and are likely only to diminish in the coming years.

SIOBHAN'S EARLY IDEAS OF CAMPING

A drawing Siobhan did when she was 4 years old. All the basics are there, in one-word sentences.

In the midst of her busy summer (she had lots of time with friends, a week of school-inspired volunteer hours, two weeks of a theatrical day-camp, music lessons, and other adventures and trips) we managed to schedule a three-day holiday at a provincial park 90 minutes from our home.

The two of us – just the two of us – had never been camping together before.

The day before we left I checked out the sorrowfully underused tent that I have owned for about 25 years (not mouldy and apparently still usable, I was pleased to see), found my old propane stove, and assembled some sleeping supplies. My daughter's tasks included overseeing the food and making lists of things so that we didn't forget anything. "I'm good at organizing and making lists, Dad. I'll take care of that!"

She planned out each of the meals and then we went shopping together to make sure we had all the food, drinks and cooking supplies we needed. As we packed up the car, she kept her eye on everything. Sunblock, flashlight, marshmallows, pots and pans – all were methodically checked off on her list with a large red felt pen.

We each packed a book. She packed *Home Truths,* by Jill MacLean, about a teenager who comes to some moments of self-knowledge through family and friends, and I packed Virgil's *Georgics,* hoping that reading Virgil among the trees would aid my understanding of his take on bees and farming and the virtues of work.

We chose a campsite with no water or electricity. The days were sweltering and the tent sloped a bit, but the campsite we were assigned was in a shady spot and was not too crowded out by other campsites and other campers.

We spent one of the days swimming in the Elora Quarry and another tubing down the Grand River – a perfect activity in the heat of the mid-day sun. Through clumsiness or foolishness, I managed to get tipped out of my inner tube and into the rapids three times. My daughter found it all very entertaining – of course she would, since she was never once tipped out of her inflated ride through the river's steep canyon walls.

CAMPING WITH VIRGIL

The copy of Virgil's *Georgics* I took with us on our camping trip.

The rest of the days we passed chunks of time making meals, reading and then in the evenings building a fire, roasting marshmallows and playing cards until it was too dark to see.

Sitting at the campsite's picnic table or on the little camping chair we brought with us, Siobhan whipped through her book pretty quickly. At one point she showed me the remains of a bug that had been flattened in its pages. "Look, Dad, a little flattened green body ... and then a squish of blood."

The paperback volume of Virgil that I brought came in handy thwapping mosquitoes in the tent, and there are various mementoes from our few days of camping in its pages: a crinkled, brownish corner where I dropped it on the ground, a few smudges from the grey-black ash that floated up from the fires that we built, and – courtesy of the squirrels scampering in the trees high above our heads – a few bits of pine and cedar bark that fell onto the open pages as I read.

We were never too far from our normal lives. My daughter and I listened to songs from our electronic devices on the drive to the campsite, and she checked her email on the ride back into the city, but we still managed the cooking of our meals out of doors, the mechanics of assembling and disassembling the tent, and the thrill of river rapids carved tens of thousands of years ago.

And we talked about stuff: the nastiness of the mosquitoes and black flies, about the sound of the river and the screams of laughter from the other people in tubes that we could hear from just beyond our campsite, and about the proper technique to fabricate out of graham crackers, chocolate chips and blackened marshmallows the perfect s'mores.

The preceding summer we had an even more spur-of-the-moment adventure. One warm Saturday morning we went for a drive in the car. Nothing too extravagant – I just thought it might be nice to head off and perhaps go grab an ice cream cone or head to the boardwalk at the other side of town and go for a walk there. A few minutes into the ride I asked Siobhan if she had any ideas for where we should go or what she would like to do. "Dad, let's go on a real adventure. Maybe to a place we've never been before. Maybe stay overnight somewhere." I was a bit surprised at her suggestion and pulled the car over to talk through her idea. We spoke for a few minutes and then decided, sure, let's do that. I said that maybe we should head back and pick up our toothbrushes and a change of clothes, but that was clearly not part of her plans. "Let's just head out. Now. We can buy toothbrushes along the way." So we headed for the highway and started to drive west.

We drove for about an hour, first along the main highway and then headed south along the secondary roads that encircle the western end of Lake Ontario. A few months earlier, Siobhan had used her music recording equipment to record a few songs on a CD, which she played on a portable CD player she had somehow rigged up through the cassette player in the old Honda. She was playing her new technology (new ways of listening) through the connections and wires of the old technology (old ways of listening). We opened all the windows of the car as wide as they would go and yelled to each other over the music and the rushing sounds of the wind and the rumbles made by the cars and the trucks that we passed or that passed us.

VOCABULARY CHECKLIST

hell – n. Tartarus
old – adj. aetate provectus
value – n. pretium
virtue – n. virtus
young – adj. parvus

PRACTICING THE LANGUAGE

Our families are built upon stories and absences.
Gentes nostrae de fabulis et itineribus componuntur.

After a while we saw a discount store along the highway and popped in. We bought a spare shirt for each of us, a package of five "Dr. Fresh Dailies" toothbrushes, a small tube of toothpaste, one treat for her (coloured jujubes) and one for me (chocolate-covered almonds). The total cost was about 11 dollars. And then we headed back into the car. Although Siobhan had wanted to go to a place we had never been before, I told her about a small town called Niagara-on-the-Lake that I had been to several times before, that was a really cute town, and that I thought she would like. So we headed there. About 10 minutes outside of town we stopped at a motel along the side of the road, checked in and left our meagre belongings.

Once the site of an Indian village, the town was settled toward the end of the American Revolution by Loyalists who had come to Upper Canada, then under the control of the British. In 1781 the British government purchased the land from the Mississauga Indians for 300 suits of clothing and later, during the War of 1812, American forces captured and later destroyed the town, before finally withdrawing.

WORDS IN FLIGHT

Verba volant, scripta manent.
Words fly away, writings remain.

– Words spoken to the Roman
Senate by Caio Titus

Siobhan and I walked among these histories, along the banks of the Lower Niagara River, and then meandered among the various touristy shops of the town. When we got hungry we stopped at a small restaurant. After dinner we bought ice cream cones, walked around some more and then headed back to the motel room. We watched TV for a half-hour or so and then slept. In the morning we headed back into town for breakfast, and then back onto the highway and home.

On the drive back we talked about the music we were listening to, about the passing landscape, and about whatever else sifted through our minds and our memories. I was also thinking about how I never got a chance to go for a similar drive with my dad, and about how happy I was to have these fleeting moments with my daughter. The drive back home was filled with random words and pleasant thoughts that evaporated into the rumbling noise of the traffic and the rushing aeriforms of the wind.

CHAPTER THIRTEEN

HIGH SCHOOL CONFIDENTIAL

"You say that you are beautiful and young."
Martial, *Epigrams*

"Don't opt out – you'll be safer in a crowd!"
Ovid, *Cures for Love*

S INCE MY FIRST CONVERSATION with Siobhan's Latin teacher, Matthew Skinner, I have been anticipating – with equal parts excitement and anxiety – the Ontario Students Classics Conference. For many of the Latin students at Humberside, the conference is, according to Matthew, the highlight of their year.

I always thought that Siobhan would be participating in the three-day conference, and that would give me a good excuse to attend as a tag-along, chaperoning parent. But a few months before the conference she says she has decided not to attend – "I just have too many other things going on, Dad" – and so here I am in the curious position of attending as a parent chaperone, even though my daughter is not at the conference.

SIOBHAN'S LATIN TEACHER

Matthew Skinner (on the left) in situ in the Humberside Latin classroom.

I immediately got more nervous and started to lose any enthusiasm I had.

"Turnip, I am really not sure I want to do this anymore! How can I go if you aren't going?"

"Dad, you'll have fun. Don't worry about it so much. You'll be fine."

"What am I supposed to do – pretend I'm a teacher, pretend I'm a high school student? What if people ask me why I'm there? What am I supposed to tell them? What if they ask me: 'So … why are you here … if your kid isn't'?"

"Stay positive, Dad. Don't be so insecure. Once it starts, it'll be okay."

"Are you sure?"

"Yes, I'm sure. It will be good. You'll have fun."

"Really?"

"Yes!"

"Okay … okay."

So I headed off with one other parent chaperone (her daughter was, of course, attending), three teachers from Humberside (in addition to Matthew there was Laura Menard, who teaches Classic Civilization and Choir; and Stephen Low, who was the Latin teacher at Humberside until he retired some years ago), and 45 students on a big, yellow school bus.

Fortunately Siobhan kept up a supportive pitter-patter of text messages, which started while the bus was still heading to the conference:

"How are things going?" she asked.

"How is the bus ride?" she asked.

"How many kids are there?" she asked.

"Have fun :) xo," she told me.

She tried to keep my spirits up.

I tried not to feel too despondent.

My dorm room was a cinder-block box. Concrete floor. Concrete walls. Concrete ceiling. It was 9 feet x 9 feet (I measured it). There was one humming fluorescent light in the room. There were no hangers in the tiny closet. The bed was a small slab of foam on a piece of plywood. The light above the sink in the communal bathroom did not work. The door on the communal toilet did not close properly. I had clearly forgotten the charms of living in a university dorm.

The conference, hosted by Brock University in St. Catharines, welcomed several hundred students, teachers and chaperones from 17 schools across the province. This was the 44th annual conference and despite an overall waning of Latin studies across Ontario over the past couple of decades, the

SO SAYS QUINTILIAN, THE GREAT EDUCATOR OF THE ROMANS

"We excuse our sloth under the pretext of difficulty."

"Our minds are like our stomachs – they are whetted by the change of their food, and variety supplies both with fresh appetite."

"Those who wish to appear wise among fools, among the wise seem foolish."

enthusiasm among all participants seemed at a fever pitch. Here were male and female high school students tossed together for a few days, bursting with interest in their chosen academic pursuit and also of course bursting with their naturally inquisitive hormonal excitements, all away from the familiar turf of home and school.

There were several dozen academic competitions, which included sight translations in Latin and Greek, and various tests on mythology, Roman history, Latin grammar and classical geography. There were also a wide assortment of athletic and creative activities, including Discus Ultimus (otherwise known as Ultimate Frisbee), an archaeological dig, school displays that included jewellery and sculpture, a sort of Latin "Reach For the Top" called Quaerite Summa, a fashion show, and Certamen Navale (dinghy races at the aquatic centre).

For the live performance competition a couple of Humberside students, Oobie Elliot and Jonathan Benedict, sang a rousing Latin song they had composed, based on the One Direction hit "One Thing." Arguably the top boy-band in the world right now, One Direction is a source of breathless devotion for many teens around the world. The band, spawned by Simon Cowell of *American Idol* and *The X Factor* fame, have over 5 million followers on Twitter, including many of Siobhan's friends (but not, interestingly, Siobhan). Students, in ancient times and our own, adapt what they are compelled to learn to their own interests and this One Direction song in Latin was met with screams of encouragement and much laughter by the assembled members of the audience and assorted fans. Here are their lyrics (before the vocabulary and grammar had been corrected by a Latin teacher):

> attenti abstinere [I have tried to hold back]
> sed amor corripit me [but "love" overcomes me]
> cygnus, imber vel bos [swan, shower, or ox]
> conversor semper fatuus [I always act foolish]
>
> dejectus ab amore [I have been shot by love]
> cupide cognoscit me [Cupid knows me]
> ego nunquam obsisti [I have never resisted]
> pulcherrimam feminam [a very beautiful woman]
>
> exedi omnino [I consumed/ate entirely]
> matrem tuum [your mother]
> nesciens nominem suum [without even knowing her name]
> sum aegrotissime [I am incredibly sick (in the head)]
>
> (et!) exi, exi, (exi) mei capiti [get out, get out, get out of my head]
> (et!) gere meam armam [and bear my arms]

nesci, nesci, nesci-i-i-o [I don't know, I don't know, I don't know]
qui explicare Iuni [explain to Juno]
quoinodo hic accidit [how this has happened]

oraclum auguravit [the oracle prophesized]
prosternar ab meo filio [that I will be overthrown by my son]
nolovi imitari patrem meum [I did not want to imitate my father]
requisivi arcere id [I needed to prevent it]

To demonstrate to the judges that they had a solid understanding of the ancient underpinnings of their song, the students provided this mythological backgrounder:

"Zeus was sleeping with Metis. An oracle of Gaea told him that Metis would bear him a daughter, and then a son, and that the son would grow up and overthrow him (as Zeus did to his own father). To prevent this from happening, Zeus ate Metis before she could give birth. He didn't realize that she was pregnant at the time, and so he ended up absorbing Athena as well. After however much time had passed, Zeus developed a headache and had to go to Hephaestus to split his skull open. Athena then emerged, fully formed, from his head."

The Humberside song did not win the competition, but it was fun to see a couple of energetic high school boys – guitar and hair flailing, hips gyrating, their voices mustering up a sort of pseudo-classical emotion – while they belted out a song in Latin as though it was the most natural thing in the world. That the song

WEARING LATIN WITH PRIDE

A T-shirt worn by a student of the University of Toronto Schools. The school's motto is: "As the tree, so the branch." Words below are Latin for "Sextus is a bad student."

was about sex and competition and questioning and headaches helped as well, I think.

One of the highlights of the conference was the final athletic event, a chariot race, in which about a dozen well-engineered and intricately decorated chariots were pulled by two student-horses at significant speed around a circular roadway. The charioteers hung on for dear life, crouching down to stay more aerodynamic, as the crowds cheered and the athletic horses raced at top speed around the circuit.

As befits any high school gathering where teenaged hormones are tingling and ready to explode, there was a pompa – a ceremonial procession, with everyone in costume: togas for the males and Latin-inspired evening wear for the females – which was then followed by a banquet and awards ceremony. The event was capped by a dance with a DJ playing loud, bacchanalian music. Some students dove or bounced or jumped into the middle of the seething mash-up of bodies, while others looked on apprehensively, gauging the perfect time and spot to tentatively enter the fray.

THE BALD EGO

Here I am at the conference, trying to look as Ciceronian as possible, with student Cameron Grenville holding the Humberside Collegiate Institute eagle standard.

Over the course of the conference I had the opportunity to speak with a lot of teachers and chaperones, as well as students from various schools, about their interest in Latin and their reasons for attending the conference.

After breakfast one day as I wandered the halls considering that this high school life I was experiencing was not all that different from the lives of adults – pretty similar worries, affections, insecurities – I walked by a few Humberside students sitting on the floor quizzing each other. When I asked what they were doing, one student told me: "We're just heading off for the derivatives exam." It took me a moment to realize that their exam had nothing to do with financial derivatives (no mention of credit default swaps or forward contracts, the source of so much creation and destruction of wealth in our current economy), or with mathematical derivatives (no mention of calculus or functions, and how quantities change in response to one another), but rather Latin derivatives (how words are formed from other words, as, for example, how the English word "derive" derives from the Latin "derivativas.")

I also had the opportunity to speak with Eugene Di Santi, the force of Latin at the University of Toronto Schools, one of the most academically challenging schools in North America. He had been teaching Latin for 32 years and had been attending this conference for 20 years. "Latin is a game of logic," he told me. "It's like a computer game for many students, with its rules and requirements." Surrounded by several students assembling his school's

FACING UP TO THE PAST

Caroline Tucker, a student at Park Tudor School in Indianapolis, and a recent president of the National Junior Classical League, when I asked her why it is important to study Latin in the age of Facebook: "The study of Latin is more than just learning the grammar and the vocabulary, it's also about exposure to a culture which shapes our everyday lives. Our language, literature, government system and arts are all influenced by Classical culture. ... This study allows me to evaluate future plans with an eye toward the past."

display – which featured historical maps, documents and constructions related to ancient history – he said that teens love "systems" and that Latin gives them a sense of both creativity and power. "I put a Latin word on the board and then ask them to play with it, to figure out what it means, and they love it."

One day over lunch I met Padraig O'Cleirigh, one of the judges for the academic portions of the conference. He had studied Latin as a kid in Ireland and now teaches Latin at the University of Guelph.

"I began to study Latin in September 1954 … with the Christian Brothers in Dundalk, Ireland," he later told me in an email. "I was all but 12 at the time and excited to be learning a new language – it was my first after the acquisition of Irish, which I had started in 1948. What I remember most

strongly about the beginning is the glow of enthusiasm in the eyes of a number of my fellow students when they said the new word *puella* – Latin for 'girl'. Though I was not insensitive to literary expression even then, I had had no experience as yet of single words presenting the things they so marvelously signified."

Two years later, Padraig went on to study at the Redemptorist College in Limerick, where he started to read Tacitus. "My teacher mentioned Tacitus as the most difficult prose writer in Latin, and therefore the most frustrating to make sense of, but that once you saw how much he could express in few words, you felt you had to stand on your desk and cheer! This revealed to me a level of enthusiasm for the language beyond what I had felt before."

SOMETIMES JUST TO PARTICIPATE IS TO WIN

I successfully participated in the conference and I have my ribbon to prove it.

After taking his BA in Ancient Classics at University College Galway, Padraig made his way to Canada, where he became Head of Classics in the School of Languages and Literatures at the University of Guelph. He regularly engages in impromptu conversations on the web in Latin, and he also attends Latin-only academic conferences.

"I regularly recommend that my intermediate Latin students read contemporary news items in *Nuntii Latini Universi*, a sort of *Huffington Post* in Latin, at ephemeris.alcuinus.net, as a prior step to conversation about today's affairs," he told me. And he attends the high school Latin conference "to admire the level of competence achieved by many high school students in translating and enunciating Latin. I hope that some of them will some year find their way into my advanced Latin classes."

Wandering around the conference and being surrounded by students and teachers for three days got me thinking about how kids learn, about how adults learn, and about how to sustain the idea of what is now widely known as life-long learning.

How high school Latin is taught also came up in an interview I later did with the Honourable Michael Meighen, a lawyer, former senator, now chancellor of McGill University, and the grandson of Canada's ninth prime minister, the Right Honourable Arthur Meighen. Michael remembers with some affection studying high school Latin at Trinity College School in Port Hope, Ontario, in the mid-1950s. He noted that his teacher, Geoff Dale, "employed a variety of innovative techniques to engage the interest of his teenage students – no mean feat, I can assure you. One of his methods was to pin up contemporary cartoons on the classroom notice board with the captions in Latin!" The language, Michael noted, "has played some role in improving my language skills – both written and spoken – both of which are of great importance to a lawyer and in public life." And he also enjoyed, as high school students do today, hearing about the "antics" of various Roman emperors.

In a blog post, "Kindergarten is the Model for Lifelong Learning," on edutopia.org, Mitchel Resnick says that kindergarten has always been "a place for telling stories, building castles, painting pictures, making friends, and learning to share." Resnick is the head of the Lifelong Kindergarten group at the MIT Media Lab, and he has a lot of wise things to say on the topic of how we learn. Of particular concern, he says, is how "In today's kindergartens, children are spending more and more time filling out worksheets and drilling on flash cards. In short, kindergarten is becoming more like the rest of school." He believes the opposite needs to happen:

> We should make the rest of school (indeed, the rest of life) more like kindergarten. What's so special about kindergarten? As kindergartners playfully create stories, castles, and paintings with one another, they develop and refine their abilities to think creatively and work collaboratively, precisely the abilities most needed to achieve success and satisfaction in the 21st century.

Edutopia is one of the initiatives of The George Lucas Educational Foundation (yes, that George Lucas, of *Star Wars* and *Indiana Jones* fame). As Lucas says, "Education is the foundation of our democracy," and he notes that "Project learning, student teams working cooperatively, children connecting with passionate experts, and broader forms of assessment can dramatically improve student learning. New digital multimedia and telecommunications can support these practices and engage our students."

Lucas remembers that "My own experience in public school was quite frustrating. I was often bored." I can certainly sympathize. I remember being quite bored in Grade 10 English. One day after class I went up to the teacher, Sr. Dickinson, and told her that I was bored and it seemed to me that other students were also bored. I suggested a few ways that she could improve the class – by talking more about contemporary literature and by involving students in more active ways in what was being taught. Well, that didn't work out too well. I was kicked out of class for two weeks. I still have the letter that the principal, Br. Bucher, wrote to my mother, about how I have to apologize to Sr. Dickinson and to him, blah blah blah. (Despite my absence from the class for two weeks, I still won the English Award that year.)

VOCABULARY CHECKLIST

chariot – n. currus
concrete – adj. concretus
name – n. nomen
student – n. litterarum studiosus
zeal – n. studium

PRACTICING THE LANGUAGE

Adults and children often have the same concerns.
Saepe fit ut parentes et liberi eadem curent.

Reading about what Resnick and Lucas have to say, recalling my own experience in my Grade 10 English class, and finding myself happily talking with high school students studying the classics, I begin to think that my presence at the conference, and this quixotic desire I have to learn a bit of Latin, are not so misplaced after all.

Many parents fear what their kids may be learning from their peers, but the students I saw at this conference were quite good at self-regulating, self-entertaining and self-learning. Of course there are problems with drugs and alcohol and bullying at Siobhan's school, and most other high schools. But so too there is a lot of support and learning and healthy experimenting with the way people and society and the world operate.

And perhaps there is some benefit to having girls and boys study together, both inside and outside the classroom. Mary Beard, the distinguished classicist, told me that when she was learning Greek she noticed that the line numbers in the margins of the text she was reading sometimes jumped "from 1,100 to 1,105 in only two lines." It was only later when her class went for a joint lecture at the local boys' school that she discovered "the truth" – that the text the girls were using "had cut out the dirty bits."

Throughout the conference I kept thinking about Ovid's *Metamorphoses*. High school students are caught in a few fundamental moments of change, of discovery, of experimentation, of learning. They embody the liminal, scattering wisdom of Ovid's central text better than they can possibly appreciate. For a teenager, the world is perhaps at its most inexplicable. There is a hunger in every teenager, even though they may not know why they are hungry, or what they are hungry for, or what will result once this hunger is temporarily satisfied. It is a challenging time for both teenagers and their parents. And parents sometimes forget that explorers and artists and teenagers who have not yet found what they are looking for can be anxious and difficult and disjointed. Parents, regrettably, often forget that they too were once teenagers.

EVERLASTING FRIENDSHIP

Amicitiae nostrae memoriam spero sempiternam fore.

I hope the memory of our friendship will be everlasting.
– Cicero

The moments from the conference that I will perhaps always remember – more than the lively sessions of Quaerite Summa, more than the toga that I was somehow convinced to wear for the pompa, more even than the chariot race – was witnessing 45 Humberside students at the end of the day squeezed into an area 15 feet x 15 feet (I measured it) listening to music, talking and singing at the top of their lungs, drinking pop, eating chips and generally reveling in their shoutmost shoviality. Long after I headed off to my monastic concrete box to sleep on a slab of foam, the students continued to talk and sing and laugh, late into the evening and on into the early hours of the next day.

CHAPTER FOURTEEN

LATIN IS DEAD, LONG LIVE LATIN

"All bodies of matter are in motion."
Lucretius, *The Nature of Things*

"Is Latin in fact dead? Is death necessarily forever?"
Joseph Farrell, *Latin Language and Latin Culture*

EVERY YEAR THERE ARE ABOUT 150,000 students worldwide who take the National Latin Exam sponsored by the American Classical League and the National Junior Classical League. Students from all 50 states, as well as from various other countries, including Australia, Canada, China, Iran, Poland, New Zealand, Taiwan and Zimbabwe participated in a recent exam. The questions range from the pretty simple:

Quis est dues Rōmānus in pictūrā?
a) Jupiter b) Apollo c) Cupid d) Mars?
(97 percent knew that C is the correct answer.)

To the ferociously difficult:

Etruscī tumulōs <u>mortuōrum hūmandorum grātiā</u> extrūxērunt.
a) with thanks for their buried dead
b) to bury their dead
c) after burying their dead
d) to honor their dead with burial
(Only 14 percent knew that B is the correct answer: a smaller percentage than if everyone who answered merely guessed.)

Now I know that 150,000 is not a huge number, but it's important to remember that most students who study Latin around the world do not take the NLE. Siobhan and all of her close friends did not take the exam. In fact, no Humberside students, in any grade, take the NLE. So 150,000 must be a small fraction of the total number of international Latin students.

For this book I interviewed 15-year-old Josef Zink, who attends a high school, Gymnasium mit Schülerheim Hohenschwangau, not far from the storied Neuschwanstein castle in Bavaria, southern Germany. In addition to his native German, Josef studies English, Latin and French. "Stultus!" (foolish, silly) is his favourite Latin word ("I think that's a funny word," he says) and he likes the story of those wolf-friendly young men, Romulus and Remus.

I also interviewed Egill Örn Jónsson, who studied Latin while attending high school at Menntaskólinn á Akureyri in northern

LIVING/DYING LATIN

Helen Keeley, interviewed earlier, remembers how she and her fellow students used to adapt the cover of their high school Latin textbook. "Anyone who took Latin in an Ontario high school in the 1960s will be familiar with this defacement," she says.

Iceland. Latin was no longer part of the curriculum, but he and a class-mate wanted to study the language, and the assistant principal, Jón Már Héðinsson, told them that if they could gather 15 students, he would help them find a teacher. They found enough students interested "without too much trouble" and soon after were studying the language. Egill now works for an international software and technology services company. "I can't say Latin has helped me much with my current work," he says, but it is useful in seeing "how the different Latin-based languages relate to each other." And Egill notes Latin-based wisdom on the grand and the small scale: "On the grander scale how some languages still maintain noun declension (like Icelandic) while others have through time been simplified (like English). And on the smaller scale, seeing certain words being so similar, like father – pater – faðir (English/Latin/Icelandic)."

Perhaps Egill's biggest learning was the "why" and the "how" of the world: "For me remembering and knowing is all about understanding. Understanding why something is makes it easy for me to remember *how* it is," he says.

And I met Livia, a 12-year-old girl who is studying Latin in Grade 7 at her local New York City school, MS.54 (Booker T. Washington) on W. 107th St. "I decided to take Latin because, of all the language teachers, the Latin teacher was my favorite," she told me. "I thought it would help me with other languages in the future. Also I enjoy history and at my school we also learn some Roman History in Latin." For her Latin vocab quizzes she sometimes studies by exchanging text messages, in Latin, with a fellow student. Here is one of her exchanges with a fellow student.

TWITTER & LATIN

"Twitter is made for Latin, and Latin is made for Twitter, because in 140 characters you have to say precisely what you want to say." Msgr. Daniel Gallagher, Vatican Latinist, on the Pope's Latin tweets. The Pope has over 225,000 followers of his Latin-language tweets.

Me: Salutationes
Him: salve
Me: Quid agis?
Him: bene ago, quid agis?
Me: bene ago
Him: ubi habitas?
Me: habito in urbe Novo Eberaco. Quid est tibi praenomen?
Him: Mihi praenomen est Oliver. Amasne equos?
Me: ???
Him: do u like horses
Me: ohhh cuz we have do u like horses and gladiators so i was confused. but...bene equos
Me: g2g
Him: bi
Me: c ya tomorrow
Him: yup bibi

When I asked her if studying Latin by texting was helping her learn the language, she told me that it helped her learn "context." And she told me she had just received a "99%!" on her most recent vocab quiz.

I also got the opportunity to hear opera singer Rachel Krehm sing (in various pieces, including *La Voix Humaine* – by Francis Poulenc and Jean Cocteau), and then ask her a few questions about her study of Latin. Rachel is the granddaughter of Bill Krehm, the 100-year-old economy-minded businessman I wrote of earlier. She studied Latin for three years during her high school years at Branksome Hall: "I wanted to take Latin because I was interested in singing and languages and I knew that studying Latin would help with my studies in French and Italian." She found out later "that it helped with German too, because of the grammar, declensions and all. Latin helped with my vocab and comprehension in other languages." Sounds like pretty good training for an opera singer who is often asked to sing in other languages.

Rachel also spoke about her study methods:

ANCIENT TECHNOLOGY STILL IN USE

Roman roadway and floor, still in fine functioning shape today. I sometimes wonder, even with our advanced technology, how many of the roads and floors we build today will still be of functional use 2,000 years from now.

I used cue cards to study for exams and I remember having a pile that must have been about six feet tall if you stacked them all up. In my final year … most of our work was in translating actual Latin authors like Virgil, Caesar, Ovid, etc. On the final exams we were required to be able to give a translation for anything that we had translated in the semester. Essentially this meant that I had to memorize about 500 lines of Latin poetry in both Latin to recognize the section and its English translation. This type of exercise helped me so much in the type of work that I do now as a singer.

And there was some enjoyment, to accompany the six-foot stack of cue cards: "We had a lot of fun in Latin class too, like watching *Spartacus*."

As I mentioned way back in Chapter 2, I have started to see Latin everywhere. And this passing year has not lessened my sightings. Perhaps I am only finding what I am seeking (as the saying goes: when you have a hammer in your hand, everything looks like a nail), but it does seem that Latin is far from dead.

Some years ago, so the apocryphal story goes, U.S. Secretary of State Henry Kissinger asked Chinese Premier Zhou Enlai for his assessment of the French Revolution. The Premier responded: "It's too early to tell." Perhaps the same could be said of Latin. How is it possible to fully assess the language – and the institutions, literature and ideas that it helped nourish – when it is still very much alive and in flux?

As I mentioned earlier, Latin, like all languages, is a technology, a tool. It is a way of seeing the world that has become, over the centuries, so integrated into the large and small arcs of our lives that we simply discount it, we pay it no attention. We stop wondering about it because it is no longer new. Latin, as we know, has helped shape 60 percent of all English words: how is it possible to acknowledge a tool that we use 60 percent of the time? Oxygen makes up about 65 percent of human bodies, but that doesn't mean we think about oxygen 65 percent of the time. Latin, it is fair to say, is like our linguistic oxygen – it is the empowering energy that enables a lot of stuff to happen. Nicholas Ostler says that Latin "has been too central to be noticed." It is, he says, like the air we breathe.

A page from the Latin website ephemeris. alcuinus.net on the discovery of the Higgs boson, for people who want a sense of history when they read about cutting-edge science.

After discussing how Latin continues to live on in the Romance languages (French, Spanish, Italian, Portuguese, and Rumanian) and in the non-national forms (Provençal, Catalan, Sardinian, Rhaeto-Romansh, and Dalmatian) Mario Pei sums up his argument with two specific linguistic examples:

> "Good bread" is *bonus panis* in Latin, *bon pain* in French, *buen pan* in Spanish, *buon pane* in Italian, *bom pão* in Portuguese, *bun pâine* in Rumanian. "One thousand" is *mille* in Latin, French and Italian, *mil* in Spanish and Portuguese, *mie* in Rumanian.

The spoken language of Rome lives on, not only in the foreign tongues which, like English, have adopted it in part and adapted it to their modern

NICE WORK, IF YOU CAN GET IT

According to Mario Pei, the Italian-American linguist (he could speak about 40 different languages) more than half of all words adopted into English from Latin have changed their meanings over the years, sometimes quite drastically. Here is a very nice example:

- The word "nice" comes originally from the Latin "nescius" (meaning "ignorant").
- In 1290, the word "nice" was first taken to mean foolish or stupid or senseless.
- In 1366, Chaucer uses the word to mean lascivious or wanton.
- By the 1400s it meant extravagant or flaunting.
- In the 1500s it came to mean strange, rare or uncommon.
- In the 1600s it meant slothful or lazy.
- Other meanings for the word include: modest, shy, refined, thin, critical, doubtful, and attentive.
- Not until the late 1700s did the word come to mean agreeable or delightful, which is the way we choose to use the word today.

As the *Oxford English Dictionary* states, considering how often the word changed its meaning over the years: "In many examples from the 16th and 17th centuries it is difficult to say in what particular sense the writer intended it to be taken."

So if you want to ridicule, insult, shock or compliment someone (perhaps all at the same time) tell them: "Nice job!"

needs but also in its numerous and picturesquely diversified descendants.

So there we have it. Latin is like good bread that we consume with hunger and pleasure, and it has spawned 1,000 descendants, each one of them, in Pei's marvellous phrase, picturesquely diversified.

Or how about this, if you're still wondering: "is it is, or is it ain't dead?" Of course Latin, as spoken by Cicero and written by Tacitus, is dead. So too my grandparents and my parents are dead. But Latin, and I, live on in a variety of ways. We are all shaped, influenced, pushed forward by the insight and ignorance that comes before us. Without Latin, the English language would not be what it is. Without my grandparents and parents I would not be here. And neither would Siobhan.

After Siobhan had finished her academic year (and received a 100% in Latin on her report card, I am very pleased to report!) I decided to design a celebratory Janus coin for use in this book. I used:

FILIAPATERLIBERCLEOPATRAMMXIV
[FILIA / PATER / LIBER / CLEOPATRA / MMXIV]
[Daughter / Father / Book / Cleopatra / 2014]

to encircle the joined profiles that have been the graphic element starting each of the chapters of this book. I also started to buy a few Roman coins off of eBay. Of course I cannot afford numismatic-quality coins with the sharp image of Cleopatra or Augustus on them. But I did manage to pick up a few coins, for about $40 to $90 each, with the relatively sharp images of some of the emperors stamped on them, including Tiberius, Claudius, Nero and Hadrian.

I also purchased an URBS ROMA coin, issued by Constantine the Great between 330 and 334 CE. These coins – which show the pagan, helmeted Roma on the obverse, and Romulus and Remus wolf-suckling on the reverse – would still have been shiny and new when Constantine converted to Christianity on his deathbed in 337. This decision by Constantine immediately elevated the place of Christianity in both the Western and Eastern Empires and changed the religious monologue/dialogue/multilogue (call it what you will) forever afterwards. Constantine's conversion decision, of course, had a direct affect on my mother's decision 1,619 years later to continue having kids, including her ninth, me. Although I'm not sure I agree with everything my Emperor-friend Constantine might have done in his life (propagating horrific civil wars, producing obsessive and extensive propaganda campaigns, being complicit in probably the most severe persecution of Christians in Roman history earlier in his career), I am thankful that Constantine's nascent Christianity had a direct influence on my mom to follow one of the teachings of the Roman Catholic faith and have as many kids as she could, even if she might not have articulated it as simply or as baldly as I do here.

And I bought a few really inexpensive coins – so old that they have carbuncles and discolourations on them, a form of historical lichen that has slowly accreted over the centuries and that make them now all but impossible to read. Some of them have just a few letters that are still legible, or they have a faint outline of a cornucopia or a head or a legionary standard. Now I always carry one of these coins with me in my pocket, as a simple reminder of how history can speak to us now – across the years and through the bronze wrinkles of a simple, pedestrian coin – if we let it.

British journalist and author Toby Young (he wrote *How To Lose Friends & Alienate People*, later made into a movie of the same name starring Kirsten Dunst and Megan Fox), wants to make sure we have historical context when we decide what to study. He recently wrote an article in *The Spectator*: "Forget Mandarin. Latin is the Key to Success."

VOCABULARY CHECKLIST

coin – n. nummus

example – n. exemplum

sing – v. cano

vocabulary – n. vocabulorum index

world – n. mundus

PRACTICING THE LANGUAGE

Latin continues to enrich our daily lives.
Lingua latina adhuc vitam nostram cottidianam ornat et auget.

Playfully calling Latin "dead," Young says the language is "precisely what today's young people need if they're going to excel in the contemporary world." He notes that "there is actually a substantial body of evidence that children who study Latin outperform their peers when it comes to reading, reading comprehension and vocabulary, as well as higher order thinking such as computation, concepts and problem solving."

Part of the body of evidence he musters and recommends is a 1979 paper by a teacher named Nancy Mavrogenes that appeared in an academic journal. "Summarising one influential American study carried out in the state of Iowa," Mavrogenes wrote:

In 1971, more than 4,000 fourth-, fifth- and sixth-grade pupils of all backgrounds and abilities received 15 to 20 minutes of daily Latin instruction. The performance of the fifth-grade Latin pupils on the vocabulary test of the Iowa Test of Basic Skills was one full year higher than the performance of control pupils who had not studied Latin. Both the Latin group and the control group had been matched for similar backgrounds and abilities.

Mavrogenes found that children from poor backgrounds showed particular benefit from studying Latin. Studying the language and learning about ancient Roman life opened up "new symbolic worlds," enabling kids to "grow as a personality, to live a richer life."

So perhaps the stories that Matthew Skinner tells Siobhan and her friends, and Josef Zink's enjoyment of the story of Romulus and Remus, and my affection for the tales of Ovid, have enabled us all to have a richer life. As Bishop Fonseca of Mumbai notes: when we coin words now "there is the tendency to choose new words from Latin." And as Llewelyn Morgan (quoted in Young's article) says: Latin is not just about grammar, it's also about "goddesses, gladiators and flying horses, or flying children."

VIRTUAL LATIN

A prime example of how we sometimes use the past to help define the present (and the future). The world's newest currency, the Bitcoin, invokes Latin to help provide, I guess, some historical lineage, some linguistic gravitas. Created for use on the web, Bitcoin is an open-source, digital currency that no single government owns or controls. Using peer-to-peer technology, it enables online purchases not covered by other payment systems.

Several entrepreneurs have seen the need to create physical representations of the Bitcoin – perhaps people think a physical Bitcoin in the hand is worth two virtual ones in the bush. The Casascius Bitcoin, designed by Mike Caldwell, uses a Latin phrase VIRIS IN NUMERIS ("Strength in Numbers"). He told me that Casascius is "the acronym for 'call a spade a spade' with a Latinized suffix." The Titan Mint uses a stylized and stylish Roman warrior and the Latin phrase UNUM PECUNIAE ("One Currency for All") on its Bitcoin.

Mandarin may very well be gathering in importance, but for the moment, for Siobhan and Josef and Rachel and Egill and Livia (and me), Latin is both the source and the fruition of much of the way we see the world.

Latin may be considered by some to be a dead language, but it is interesting to note that it is studied by more people now than it was in Roman times. So, what to think about Latin – its impact, its role, its many footprints? As the Mandarin-speaking Zhou Enlai might say (and as I do say): It's really too early to tell.

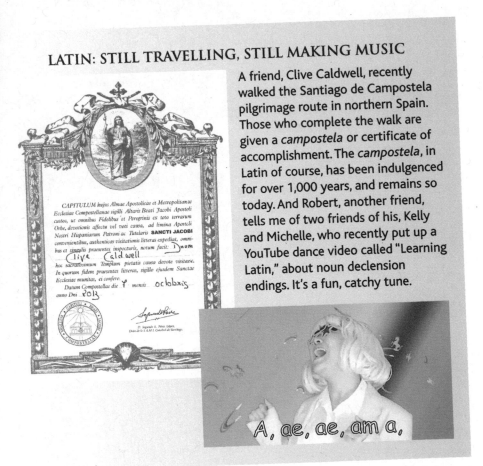

LATIN: STILL TRAVELLING, STILL MAKING MUSIC

A friend, Clive Caldwell, recently walked the Santiago de Campostela pilgrimage route in northern Spain. Those who complete the walk are given a *campostela* or certificate of accomplishment. The *campostela*, in Latin of course, has been indulgenced for over 1,000 years, and remains so today. And Robert, another friend, tells me of two friends of his, Kelly and Michelle, who recently put up a YouTube dance video called "Learning Latin," about noun declension endings. It's a fun, catchy tune.

Chapter Fifteen

ET CETERA

"All those passions and perturbations of the mind, etc."
Robert Burton, *The Anatomy of Melancholy*

"Iam liquescit / et decrescit / grando, nix et cetera."
"Now everything melts and disappears: the ice, the snow, et cetera."
Words set by Carl Orff in *Carmina Burana*

PARENTS ARE WAY TOO CLOSE to their children to notice the quotidian changes that are always, relentlessly, occurring. The million little pieces of a life that more or less meander in the same general direction, and that shape, craft and define the colour of our connected lives. The agglomeration of minikin changes that make up the larger arc of a person's life.

Depending on the age of the child, a parent gets to see many, or none, or few of these shards, these fleeting specks of the spectrum. Watching and listening to infants, they are everywhere in evidence; during the teenage years, watch and listen as parents might, the desire and impulse of the object is more toward the hidden or the private. Seldom are we fully conscious of their importance or their filiation. Every once in a while we can see the world of a child in a grain of sand, but more often what we see is a rushing and uncontrollable tumult of multitudinous grains of sand that move way too quickly and far too randomly for us to make sense of them.

It has been fun to watch Siobhan develop her gathering independence over this past year. Watching her closely – sometimes so furtively that she did not see me watching her – and recording some of what I've seen led me to recall moments of my own teen years, and it has helped me appreciate the infinite and indefinable singularity of each of us. It is too much to ask for some insight, some grand flash

SAND AND DINNER

"You don't see eternity except in the grain of sand, or history except at the family dinner table."
– James Merrill

of understanding. For me it has been sufficient to appreciate the passing adventure. In an essay on one of the *Upanishads*, Yeats talks about the importance of "dedicating all things as they pass." I first read that line when I was about 20 years old, and it has been with me whenever I've wondered how best to preserve the passing moments that I spend with Siobhan.

So what has been studied and what has been learned over the past year, through this rather quaint idea of mine to spend time studying Latin (the past) with my teenaged daughter (the present) and then writing a few words about it for her and others to read (the future)?

One thing I've learned is that I ask way too many questions. In early January (the month of looking both forward and backward) I asked Siobhan what she had learned this past year – not through the subjects she studied at school but through her travelling from the world of a young teenager to that of a mid-teenager. I was anticipating a bit of 15-year-old wisdom: disorienting or incontrovertible or maybe just silly. Instead, she responded to my hopeful question with: "What do you mean? I don't know, Dad. How come you ask me questions like that?"

Perhaps that's the same sort of answer that I would give her if she asked me what I have learned over the past year: "I don't know. Why do you ask me questions like that?"

A SAMPLER OF NATIONAL MOTTOS

Andorra: *Virtus unita fortior* (Strength united is stronger)
British Virgin Islands: *Vigilante* (Be watchful)
Canada: *A mari usque ad mare* (From sea to sea)
Gibraltar: *Nulli Expugnabilis Hosti* (Conquered by no enemy)
Monaco: *Deo juvante* (With God's help)
North Borneo: *Pergo et Perago* (I undertake and I achieve)
Panama: *Pro mundi beneficio* (For the benefit of the world)
Switzerland: *Unus pro omnibus, omnes pro uno* (One for all, all for one)
United States: In God We Trust (official);
E pluribus unum (Out of many, one) (de facto)

At the beginning of this scheme, I imagined that at the end of the academic year I would be magically transported into a world of knowledge where I could effortlessly read Virgil and Ovid in the original Latin. Nope, that hasn't happened. Not even close, although I can recognize a bunch of Latin words, and have seen much more clearly the legacy that Latin has provided English. As for declensions and derivatives and understanding the subtleties of an inflected language like Latin? Nope.

I had even entertained taking the final Grade 10 Latin test – the same test that Siobhan took to determine her final grade in the class. Matthew also suggested that I might want to take it, and that he would happily arrange it, not of course with the rest of the students, but on my own, under some minimally supervised situation. Siobhan had a certain malicious glee in her voice whenever we talked about this possibility. "That would be so good … for the book, Dad. Really! You'll get 36 percent on the final Latin test, and I'll get 96 percent! So … don't you think that would be good for the book?" Well, I chickened out – I never did take the final test. And I think her speculating on me getting 36 percent on the final test would have been pretty close to what actually happened, even if I had got in some last-minute cramming. And to add numerical insult to injury, as I mentioned earlier, her final mark was not 96 but rather 100 percent.

I also imagined that I would sense a new rumble of wisdom coursing through my blood, an understanding of how the virtual worlds of the Internet and the study of Latin, now virtually disregarded by most people, could coexist. Again, limited success. Often I only felt, Heisenberg-like, as though I was always and only just getting in the way of exactly what it was I was trying to discover or learn. Perhaps the best way I can express what I learned about these two vastly different worlds is that they can and do exist simultaneously. There are traces of Latin and Roman history in our languages and in our democracies, our cultures, our religions and our technologies. And the Internet traces out for us and delineates all of the desires, hopes and fears that have always been used to define what it is to be human. The Internet doesn't redefine what it is to be human; it merely provides a new angle with which to view the passing show. So not much wisdom or insight there: just a couple of tentative observations.

I also imagined that by studying alongside my daughter I would be better able to connect, in a fundamentally stronger way, with her as she moves through parts of her fourteenth and fifteenth year. Some "success" here, but only to a degree. If anything, I have become more closely connected to the disconnections between me and my daughter, to the differences that are slowly expanding and

THE END OF LATIN, THE BEGINNING OF LATIN DICTIONARIES

In the 11th century the first Latin dictionaries appeared, put to use by students and novices who no longer had Latin as their mother tongue.

separating us – the sort of natural and inevitable and healthy freedoms that are enabling her to truly function and flourish on her own. Perhaps I've learned that when it comes to Siobhan I cannot learn all that I want to learn.

And what, really, has Siobhan learned by studying Latin as a teenager in the era of Facebook, YouTube, Twitter and Bitcoin? Indeed, what does any student learn in Grade 10: one of those transitional grades that follows on those earlier years of blind discovery and formless experimentation; one of those grades that is not really essential for university admissions offices as they try to figure out who to admit and who to pass over? She had another good year academically, although I had confidence that was going to happen, so there really is no surprise or new wisdom there. She has learned more about her friends, about various personal changes and challenges that await her, and about the media, technology, money and all sorts of other things, none of which she needed Latin for. Perhaps what she has learned is that the past is not really past and that it continues to influence and affect the eternal now, and that, as Marshall McLuhan said, "all possible futures are contained in the present." Perhaps.

By hanging around Siobhan I was seeking some insight into the technologies that we choose to surround ourselves with – and that includes the whole gamut, from books to weapons to particle accelerators to the Internet. Some of our technologies do help us connect with the things around us: on my iPhone I use my weather app and my camera and my Twitter account and my phone constantly. And some of our technologies help us to imagine. We cannot see the Higgs boson, and we'll never see the outer reaches of our expanding 14-billion-year-old universe, but we can now imagine them better, thanks to free apps and the world of digitized knowledge that we can carry around with us in our pockets.

Within this universe of infinite ideas, there are some human basics – and this again includes the gamut, from love to discovery to storytelling to death – that seem to remain central to our lives without any intrusion or influence of technology. Two people at the core of Siobhan's life have died over the past couple of years. One was her voice and guitar teacher, Taylor Mitchell, who died at the age of 19, after she was attacked by coyotes while walking along a trail in Cape Breton, on her first music tour to publicize her first album. The other was her maternal grandfather, John, who first taught Siobhan the basics of playing the piano, and who died at the age of 78.

Although technology was a part of Siobhan building and nurturing a relationship with and an understanding of these two people (automobiles to travel, telephones to talk, recording equipment to capture developing sounds, email used to exchange information), when these two people died, Siobhan and all of the rest of us were left to deal with the absence and the silence on our own. The sympathies and the regrets and the memories that we develop, although sometimes abetted by technology, can stand on their own and sometimes have to stand on their own. Siobhan had to absorb these two fractures in her life on her own, in her own way and in her own time.

THE MANY FORMS OF ET CETERA

Etcetera, et caetera, et coetera, et cœtera, etc., &c., &/c., &e., &ct., &ca.

Like any parent, there are many days when I am sure that Siobhan is quite convinced I have nothing to teach her, or at least nothing to pass on to her that she would be naturally interested in learning. But sometimes, some few rare times, this worldview is turned on its head. Because I do some thinking and writing about visual art, and I have recently been considering the relationship between art and fashion, Siobhan (every once in a while) gets a sense, I think, of maybe-my-dad-isn't-quite-so-straight-and-quite-so-boring-as-I-thought, and even an infinitesimal particle of maybe-my-dad-actually-knows-a-bit-about-fashion.

One morning while getting ready for school she actually said to me: "Dad, I need your fashion advice."

"Ummm. OK. Are you sure? You want my fashion advice."

"Yep. OK, so I'm wearing this great new peach-coloured sweater I bought two days ago at a second-hand vintage clothing store. See the way the colour matches a stripe on my belt? See what I mean? And then I'm wearing my skinny blue jeans, although at first I thought I was going to wear my skinny black jeans, but I think the blue ones work better. And so I'm also going to wear these funky new shoes – well they're sort of new. I bought them in New York last summer but I haven't really worn them yet. See, they're mostly brown but they also have some flower stuff going on. And see, there are a few peach-coloured flowers on the shoes. So, what I'm wondering about is: is it just too much? Is there too much of a peach-peach-peach, sweater-belt-shoe thing going on? You know, yesterday I wore a black T-shirt and that seemed to work with the sweater and the belt. But today, I'm just not sure. And at school … well I just don't want it to look all too peachy. So what do you think? Is this OK?"

"Sure, I think it looks great. Very cute. And it's not too much peach."

"OK, thanks."

And so that's what she wore to school that day. Of course my advice was not much more than a marginal note of approval, but that was really all I could offer her, and it was, as it turned out, good enough for her.

I enjoy all these meandering motes of my daughter's life, these moments of what I've come to call the Daughterland. Each moment has its own wisdom and beauty and challenge, as well as its own impenetrability. When I became a father about 15 years ago, other parents started to talk to me about their favourite times with their child or children. "Oh, wait until she starts to walk – that's when the real joy is," they'd say. Or "Wait until she starts to speak – that's when things get interesting." Or "Wait until she heads off to university." Or "Wait until she gets married." Or or or. These observations became tedious quite quickly, perhaps because I so emphatically disagreed with them. Every passing moment has been marvellous – that is, full of marvels. I have said to my daughter many times that every moment I have ever spent with her – and I mean *every* moment – is better than *any* other moment I have ever had in my life, and that includes whatever moments of success or achievement or celebration that I've had. This book has been a way for me to spend a few more moments in her company.

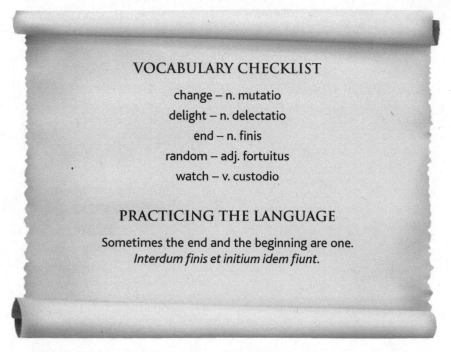

VOCABULARY CHECKLIST

change – n. mutatio
delight – n. delectatio
end – n. finis
random – adj. fortuitus
watch – v. custodio

PRACTICING THE LANGUAGE

Sometimes the end and the beginning are one.
Interdum finis et initium idem fiunt.

Reading the anti-heroic spectacles of Lucan, the mazed silliness of Plautus, and the elegant ecstasies of Horace has been fun, but the most pleasure I've had over the past year is reading Siobhan and then preserving a few of those words in a form of word-based amber. Sometimes a small, random speck of nature – a worker bee heading off on an errand, or a petal loosened from a wind-ruffled flower – will become entangled with the resin of a tree and over the millennia will be fossilized into a time-defeating chunk of translucent amber. (A quick, etceterative digression: The word "amber" originally comes to us from the Greek word "ηλεκτρον" for "electron," and from which we derive the word "electricity." From there the word flows through the Arabic "anbar" and the Medieval Latin "ambar" and the Old French "amber.") This random event – the flitting bee or the loosening petal probably never spoke about it, either to themselves or to the other bees or petals – is miraculously transformed over and through time into a gesture of unique and permanent beauty. It is impossible to shape or define, even to describe, all of the intricacies of such an ambered event. It is sufficient to look in on the event from a distance and to marvel at its simplicity, its elegance. I've been pleased over this past year to have had some of these events.

Of course there is a lot of other stuff that should go in a chapter called "Et Cetera," including Nicholas Ostler's summing-up observation: "Languages create worlds to live in." And how Thornton Wilder calls Cleopatra "Missy Crocodile" in his book *The Ides of March*. And how Mary Beard, in an encouraging moment, said in an email to me: "When you've done Latin, try a little Greek … they make a great pair." Ha! Not likely!

Going through some of the school assignments, cards and pictures that Siobhan has produced over the years (I toss this type of material into a storage box, thinking that at some point in the future Siobhan will be happy to have it) I recently came across a note that accompanied a small painting Siobhan made for me when she was 9 years old. The note captures a few moments of our shared history:

Dear Daddy: This abstract picture is a picture of all the fun edventures we have! Find a wall with your hand sticking out and mine. (That's when we got locked in the zoo!!) Find our favourite tree!! (That come's in the spring!!) Find your face being stressed because you can't play the piano, and I'm trying to teach you it!! WE HAVE HADE A LOT OF FUN TOGETher

221

BOOK OF KELLS

A page from one of the most beautiful
books ever made.

And perhaps there is room for a few more quotable words from Siobhan. One morning in the early summer, after her Grade 10 Latin class had ended, she and I were walking out of the apartment, past the spot where residents drop off books, kitchen stuff, furniture and other miscellaneous things for exchange or just to get rid of. This particular time there was just one item: a book, *Getting Pregnant.* As we passed by, Siobhan nonchalantly stated: "Hey, that's my book."

Marguerite Yourcenar, the first woman ever elected to the Academie Française, and whom I referenced earlier, talks about a sense of shared history. In her marvellous book *Memoirs of Hadrian* – which is a long letter that the aging Emperor Hadrian writes to the future emperor, Marcus Aurelius – Yourcenar writes about foreshortening or collapsing history. Writing in her "Reflections" on the composition of the book, she creates an eloquent and simple metaphor on how closely we are connected to past events: "Some five and twenty aged men, their withered hands interlinked to form a chain, would be enough to establish an unbroken contact between Hadrian and ourselves."

Utilizing that same metaphor, I can say that the life span of one 80-year-old person brings Siobhan and me back to our parents and grandparents – to New York and Newfoundland, to Ottawa and Ireland – whose faces adorn and enliven our family photo wall.

Two 80-year-old people holding hands get us back to the time of the Great Famine in Ireland and our Irish ancestors, struggling through economic hardship and wondering about a new life on the other side of the world. Sometimes, as is evident from our own family, a bout of seasickness in the 1860s

From a Roman frieze.

has the ability to shape the lives of people in what must have seemed then to be the very distant future.

Five 80-year-olds holding hands get us back to the time of Elizabeth I and Shakespeare, of the Tudor lineage that brought the Queen Regnant of England to the throne and of raucous crowds milling about at the Globe Theatre watching plays that Siobhan and I both continue to read and enjoy.

Fifteen 80-year-olds holding hands get us back to the time of Celtic scribes copying Latin texts and illustrating the vellum pages of the Book of Kells, one of the most beautiful books ever produced, which both Siobhan and I have seen, on separate visits, at its permanent home, Trinity College, Dublin.

Twenty-seven 80-year-olds holding hands get us back to the time of Caesar and Cleopatra and Mark Anthony and Augustus, of personal intrigue and civil war, of writings that still sway with profound rhetorical flourishes, and of ceremonial architecture that still impresses to this day.

Thirty-five 80-year-olds holding hands get us back to the first buds, the first flowerings of the Latin language, and the beginning of a new way of

From a coin minted during the reign of the Emperor Nerva.

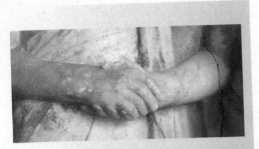

From a statue in the Glyptothek, Munich.

thinking that continues to influence our days and our stories now.

There is some delight in considering how close we are to these ancient times, and their achievements, struggles, enchantments, et cetera. Earlier I spoke about "degrees of separation." Perhaps we can also talk about chronological degrees of separation: how only five chronological degrees of separation get us back to Shakespeare and how only 27 of these degrees of separation get us back to Cleopatra. That is, it seems to me, not so many.

Presumably, these sorts of chronological connections also work when we consider the future – that a few generations from now, or a few dozen generations from now, people will talk about how what happened in the first decades of the 2000s influenced their own times. Studying the Latin language and Roman history can help enliven and energize some of these connections between the past and the future.

For me, this year of study has also enabled some pleasures of the present. I have been sharing some time – a few incidental ticks of the eternal and the transient – with my daughter, Siobhan.

ACKNOWLEDGEMENTS

WHEN I STARTED THIS BOOK I thought that it was going to be exclusively about my daughter Siobhan and me. As I told people about the idea, many mentioned their own connections to Latin and suggested further leads: "My mother studied Latin in China – she'd love to talk to you"; "My uncle is the former Bishop of Mumbai – you should talk to him"; "My daughter, who is 12, studies Latin at the local public school in New York City, and she really likes it." And so the project has expanded to accommodate a selection of these voices and observations.

Many have helped this book along. Some I have known for decades, and some I discovered and befriended because of the engendering needs and joys of this book. All warrant my specific and ongoing thanks.

As Rome is the Eternal City, Bob Shantz has been the Eternal Friend. Over the years he has been the bemused, reverend and supportive person who has had to listen to my sometimes quixotic desires, and has been present for most of the recent declines and falls.

Robert Everett-Green, orchestral in his interests and enthusiasms, with whom I have shared many inspiring and motivating conversations about all sorts of things, including some of the ancient writers invoked within these pages.

Elaine Fantham – "the *grande dame* of Latin Studies in the English-speaking world" – for her boundless wisdom, and for her many great suggestions for further reading. Because of her I almost added two additional sources of insight to the bibliography: those distinguished scholars Dalwhinnie and Lagavulin.

Rita M. Reichart, the much bejangled, has been an enthusiastic supporter of many things related and unrelated to this book, and she has connected me to various intriguing and insightful characters whom I would never have otherwise met.

Rita's good friend Suzanne Gayn, still a sprightly force at 92, has encouraged the idea of this book, and the support necessary to see it to fruition, and for that I am very thankful.

Allan Briesmaster of Quattro Books has been as supportive, helpful and encouraging as a publisher could be – he loves language and words and the ideas they engender, and he has provided an informed and crafting hand to these words. Julie McNeill, the designer, has created a strong and sympathetic graphic canvas on which these words appear. Robert Lecker, my agent, has been enthusiastic about this book from the beginning. Thanks to Maddy Curry for her sharp eye and insightful fact-checking.

And Morden Yolles, who structured and engineered many leads for me – to people, books, stories, memories, et cetera. Philanthropic by nature, Mordy also assisted this project with support at a time when it was very much needed. We share the same birthday, and I hope that when I reach my late 80s I have a similar sense of intellectual curiosity.

I would also like to thank others who provided stories, information and related other wisdoms – through letters, conversations, phone calls, emails and tweets – some of whom are quoted within these pages:

John Allemang
John Armstrong
David Bale
Leah Barrett
Mary Beard
David Beauroy
Rebecca Benefiel
Dominic Berry
Rabbi Arthur Bielfeld
Lorène Bourgeois
Terrence Bredin
Robyn Buchman
Phillip Chown
Marie Côté
Alain de Botton
Theresa de Weerd
Cookie Diestel
Lauralee Edgell
Luciana Famulski
Bishop Ferdinand Fonseca
Rivi Frankle
John Fraser
Cynthia Good
Harold Heft
Suzanne Heft
Geoffrey James
Egill Örn Jónsson
Shaista Justin
Janet Kim
Dragana Klajic
Rachel Krehm
William Krehm
Sir Harry Kroto
Hillary Kunins
Craig Laatz
Barbara Lamb
Barbara Leckie
Peter Legris

Gordon Lightfoot
Lorraine Linton
Tulu Makonnen
Rose Anne McCants
Indra Kagis McEwen
Sarah McKinnon
Susan Meech
Hon. Michael Meighen
Laura Menard
Desmond Montague
Elizabeth Montague
Linda Montross
James Morwood
Herimannus Novocomensis
Bridget O'Brien
Colleen O'Brien
Padraig O'Cleirigh
Sheilagh O'Connell
Eric Petersiel
Josephina Reichart
Simon Reichart
David Rippner
Tom Robinson
Michael Scott
Nadia Serraf
Mohamed Sheybow
Matthew Skinner
Alison Smiley
Jill Standish
Mary Stinson
Howard Swatland
Lance Talbot
Caroline Tucker
Joel Westheimer
Miriam Westheimer
Dr. Ruth Westheimer
Christa Wiehl
Josef Zink

In a reversal of the standard "Acknowledgements" sentiment: I'm pretty confident with my own words, but I can't always vouch for the opinions, memories or veracity of the others I quote within these pages.

BIBLIOGRAPHICAL SOURCES

THIS IS AN IDIOSYNCRATIC LIST of the Latin authors that I found most important for this book, and then a selection of other sources consulted or quoted. Most of the Latin sources are in English translations and a few are bilingual editions. When I enjoyed more than one translation of a particular author – sometimes because of the strength of the introduction or the notes – I listed each.

PRINCIPAL LATIN AUTHORS

Apuleius (c. 120 – c. 180 CE)
The Transformations of Lucius, Otherwise Known as The Golden Ass,
translated and with an introduction by Robert Graves. Farrar, Straus and Giroux, 2009.

Caesar (100 – 44 BCE)
The Civil War, translated and with an introduction by John Carter. Oxford World's Classics, 2008.
The Gallic War, translated and with an introduction by Carolyn Hammond. Oxford World's Classics, 2008.

Cassius Dio (c. 163 – c. 235 CE)
The Roman History: The Reign of Augustus, translated by Ian Scott-Kilvert, and with an introduction by John Carter. Penguin, 1987.

Catullus (c. 84 – c. 54 BCE)

The Poems of Catullus: A Bilingual Edition, translated and with
commentary by Peter Green. University of California, 2005.

The Poems of Catullus, translated and with an introduction by Peter
Whigham. Penguin, 1966.

Cicero (106 – 43 BCE)

On Living and Dying Well, translated and with an introduction by
Thomas Habinek. Penguin, 2012.

On Obligations, translated and with an introduction by P. G. Walsh.
Oxford World's Classics, 2008.

Political Speeches, translated and with an introduction by D. H. Berry.
Oxford, 2009.

The Republic and The Laws, translated and with an introduction by
Jonathan Powell and Niall Rudd. Oxford, 2008.

Horace (65 – 8 BCE)

Horace: The Complete Odes and Epodes, translated and with an
introduction by David West. Oxford, 2000.

The Epistles of Horace: A Bilingual Edition, translated and with an
introduction by David Ferry. Farrar, Straus and Giroux, 2001.

The Satires and Epistles of Horace, translated and with an introduction by
Smith Palmer Bovie. University of Chicago, 1959.

Juvenal (c. 55 – c. 120 CE)

The Satires of Juvenal, translated and with an introduction by Rolfe
Humphries. Indiana University, 1958.

The Sixteen Satires, translated and with an introduction by Peter Green.
Penguin, 1974.

Livy (64 BCE – 12 CE)

The Rise of Rome: Books One to Five, translated and with an introduction
by T. J. Luce. Oxford, 1998.

The Dawn of the Roman Empire: Books 31-40, translated by J. C. Yardley,
introduction by Waldemar Heckel. Oxford World's Classics, 2009.

Lucan (39 – 65 CE)

Civil War, translated and with an introduction by Susan H. Braund.
Oxford, 2008.

Lucretius (c. 100 – c. 50 BCE)
On the Nature of Things, translated by W. H. D. Rouse, revised by Martin
F. Smith. Loeb Classical Library, Harvard, 1992.
The Nature of Things, translated by A. E. Stallings, introduction by
Richard Jenkyns. Penguin, 2007.

Macrobius (5th century CE)
Saturnalia, edited and translated by Robert. A. Kaster. Loeb Classical
Library, Harvard, 2011.

Marcus Aurelius (121 – 180 CE)
*Marcus Aurelius and His Times: The Transition from Paganism to
Christianity,* with an introduction by Irwin Edman. Walter J. Black,
1945.
Meditations, translated by Martin Hammond, introduction by Diskin
Clay. Penguin, 2006.

Martial (c. 40 – c. 102 CE)
Martial's Epigrams: A Selection, translated and with an introduction by
Garry Wills. Penguin, 2008
The Epigrams, selected and translated by James Michie. Penguin, 1978.

Ovid (43 BCE – c. 18 CE)
*The Erotic Poems: The Amores, The Art of Love, Cures for Love, On Facial
Treatment for Ladies,* translated and with an introduction by Peter
Green. Penguin, 1982.
Ovid Metamorphoses, translated and notes by Charles Martin;
introduction by Bernard Knox. W. W. Norton, 2004.
Tales from Ovid, Ted Hughes. Farrar, Straus and Giroux, 1997.

Petronius (c. 27 – c. 66 CE)
Petronius: The Satyricon and Seneca: The Apocolocyntosis, translated and
with introductions by J. P. Sullivan. Penguin, 1986.

Plautus (254 – 184 BCE)
Four Comedies, translated and with an introduction by Erich Segal.
Oxford, 1998.
The Rope and Other Plays, translated and with an introduction by E. F.
Watling. Penguin, 1964.

Pliny the Elder (23 – 79 CE)
Natural History: A Selection, translated and with an introduction by John
F. Healy. Penguin, 2004.

Pliny the Younger (c. 61 – c. 112 CE)
Complete Letters, translated and with an introduction by P. G. Walsh.
Oxford, 2006.

Quintilian (c. 35 – c. 100 CE)
On the Early Education of the Citizen-Orator, translated by Rev. John Selby
Watson, introduction by James J. Murphy. Bobbs-Merrill, 1965.
Quintilian on Education, translated and with an introduction by William
M. Smail. Oxford, 1938.

Seneca (4 BC – 65 CE)
Selected Letters, translated and with an introduction by Elaine Fantham.
Oxford World's Classics, 2010.
Six Tragedies, translated and with an introduction by Emily Wilson.
Oxford World's Classics, 2010.

Suetonius (c. 70 – c. 130 CE)
Lives of the Caesars, translated and with an introduction by Catharine
Edwards. Oxford World's Classics, 2008.

Sulpicia (1st century BCE)
Six Poems, Anne Mahoney, editor. Tufts University, Perseus Digital
Library 4.0.

Tacitus (c. 56 – c. 117 CE)
Agricola and Germany, translated and with an introduction by A. R.
Birley. Oxford, 2009.
The Annals: The Reigns of Tiberius, Claudius, and Nero, translated by J. C.
Yardley and with an introduction and notes by Anthony A. Barrett.
Oxford, 2008.
The Histories, translated and with an introduction by W. H. Fyfe, revised
and edited by D. S. Levine. Oxford, 2008.

Terence (c. 184 – 159 BCE)
The Comedies, translated and with an introduction by Peter Brown.
Oxford World's Classics, 2008.

Virgil (70 – 19 BCE)

Aeneid, translated by Frederick Ahl, introduction by Elaine Fantham. Oxford, 2007.

The Aeneid, translated by Robert Fagles, introduction by Bernard Knox. Penguin, 2006.

The Aeneid, translated and with a postscript by Robert Fitzgerald. Vintage, 1990.

The Eclogues and The Georgics, translated by C. Day Lewis, introduction by R. O. A. M. Lyne. Oxford, 2009.

The Georgics of Virgil: A Bilingual Edition, translated and with an introduction by David Ferry. Farrar, Straus and Giroux, 2005.

TRANSLATION 101 –
THE BENEFITS OF SAMPLING

It may seem rather curious, but sometimes I distill and then yoke together several different translations, trying to build my own translation out of the available ones out there, adding as the spirit moves me a bit of wisdom from a Latin-English dictionary or an online translation tool. The fact is, there are often great translations of the same text, and it is always interesting to compare translations.

Here's an example of what I mean. Our age has three superior recent translations of Virgil's *Aeneid* – by Robert Fitzgerald (1983), Robert Fagles (2006), and Frederick Ahl (2007). Here is one of my favourite moments in this vast epic, from Book Nine.

The Latin is followed first by the translation by Fitzgerald, then by Fagles, then by Ahl and then by me (dependant, to state the obvious, more on my "sampling" skills than on my own Latin skills):

Nisus ait: "dine hunc ardorem mentibus addunt,
Euryale, an sua cuique deus fit dira cupido?
aut pugnam aut aliquid iamdudum inuadere magnum
mens agitat mihi, nec placida contenta quiete est."

And Nisus said:
"This urge to action, do the gods instill it,
Or is each man's desire a god to him,
Euryalus? For all these hours I've longed
To engage in battle, or to try some great
Adventure. In this lull I cannot rest."

"Euryalus,"
Nisus asks, "do the gods light this fire in our hearts
or does each man's mad desire become his god?
For a while now a craving's urged me on
to swing into action, some great exploit –
no peace and quiet for me."

"'Is it, Euryalus, gods who implant these obsessions,' said Nisus,
'Deep in our minds? Or do each individual's passions become god?
My mind's been nagging me now for a while to try battle, or something
major. It isn't the least bit content with this tranquil inertia.'"

Then Nisus asks: "Do the gods light this fire in our hearts,
or does each man's own desire become his god?
Euryalus, for some time now I've had this longing to
confront and to fight, or to attempt some great
new adventure. I can't sit still and rest in a quiet state."

I have no knowledge that would enable me to attempt anything
more than these silly little translation games, but they can be fun and
perhaps even helpful in navigating through the world of Latin, even
with a poem as "famously untranslatable" (to use Joseph Farrell's
words) as *The Aeneid*.

OTHER WORKS CONSULTED OR QUOTED

Adkins, Lesley and Roy A. Adkins. *Handbook to Life in Ancient Rome.* Oxford, 1994.

Ashenburg, Katherine. *The Dirt on Clean: An Unsanitized History.* Knopf, 2007.

Atwood, Margaret. *The Handmaid's Tale.* Houghton, Mifflin, 1986.

Bloom, Harold. *How to Read and Why.* Scribner, 2000.

Boardman, John, Jasper Griffin and Oswyn Murray, eds. *The Oxford Illustrated History of The Roman World.* Oxford, 2001.

Boswell, James. *Life of Johnson.* Oxford UP, 1976.

Bryson, Bill. *A Short History of Nearly Everything.* Anchor Canada, 2004.

——. *The Mother Tongue: English & How It Got That Way.* William Morrow, 1990.

Bunson, Matthew. *A Dictionary of the Roman Empire.* Oxford, 1995.

Busch, Wilhelm. *Max und Moritz Polyglott (deutsch, englisch, franzosisch, spanisch, italienisch, lateinisch).* Deutscher Taschenbuch Verlag, 1982.

Cahill, Thomas. *How the Irish Saved Civilization: The Untold Story of Ireland's Heroic Role from the Fall of Rome to the Rise of Medieval Europe.* Doubleday, 1995.

Cappelli, Adriano. *Dizionario di Abbreviature latine ed italiane: Sesta edizione.* Ulrico Heopli, 1985.

Carcopino, Jerome. *Daily Life in Ancient Rome,* Second Edition. New introduction and bibliographic essay by Mary Beard. Yale, 2003.

Carr, Nicholas. *The Shallows: What the Internet Is Doing to Our Brains.* Norton, 2011.

Chase, Alston Hurd, and Henry Phillips, Jr. *A New Introduction to Greek,* Third Edition. Harvard, 1961.

Clavier, Dr. Ron. *Teen Brain, Teen Mind: What Parents Need to Know to Survive the Adolescent Years.* Key Porter, 2005.

Deary, Terry. *The Horrible History of the World.* Scholastic, 2003.

de Botton, Alain. *How Proust Can Change Your Life.* Vintage International, 1997.

Dewdney, Christopher. *Soul of the World: Unlocking the Secrets of Time.* HarperCollins, 2008.

Dixon, Suzanne. *The Roman Family.* The Johns Hopkins University Press, 1992.

Dobbs, David. "Beautiful Brains: The New Science of the Teenage Brain." *National Geographic,* October 2011.

Draper, Robert. "The Late Adopters." *The New York Times Magazine,* February 17, 2013.

Drexler, Dr. Peggy. *Our Fathers, Ourselves: Daughters, Fathers, and the Changing American Family.* Rodale, 2011.

Edery, David, and Ethan Mollick. *Changing the Game: How Video Games are Transforming the Future of Business.* FT Press, 2009.

Einstein, Albert. *Relativity: The Special and General Theory.* Authorized translation by Robert W. Lawson. Three Rivers Press, 1961.

Eliot, T. S. *Four Quartets.* Faber, 1959.

Everitt, Anthony. *Augustus: The Life of Rome's First Emperor.* Random House, 2006.

———. *Cicero: A Turbulent Life.* John Murray, 2002.

Fantham, Elaine. *Roman Literary Culture: From Plautus to Macrobius.* Second edition. The Johns Hopkins University Press, 2013.

———, et al. *Women in the Classical World: Image and Text.* Oxford, 1994.

Farrell, Joseph. *Latin Language and Latin Culture from ancient to modern times.* Cambridge UP, 2001.

Finley, M. I. *The Use and Abuse of History.* Hogarth Press, 1986.

Flaubert, Gustave. *Bouvard and Pécuchet [includes the Dictionary of Received Ideas],* translated by A. J. Krailsheimer. Penguin, 1976.

Frye, Northrop. *The Educated Imagination.* Canadian Broadcasting Corporation, 1963.

Gardner, Jane F. and Thomas Wiedemann. *The Roman Household: A Sourcebook.* Routledge, 1991.

Gates, Bill. "Why America is Not a New Rome." www.thegatesnotes.com, book review dated October 21, 2010.

Gibbon, Edward. *The History of the Decline and Fall of the Roman Empire.* AMS Press / Methuen & Co., 1909.

Gilder, Louisa. *The Age of Entanglement: When Quantum Physics was Reborn.* Knopf, 2009.

Golden, Mark. *Children and Childhood in Classical Athens.* The Johns Hopkins University Press, 1993.

Graves, Robert. *I, Claudius.* Penguin, 1953.

———. *Claudius The God.* Methuen, 1986.

Hallett, Judith P. *Fathers and Daughters in Roman Society.* Princeton, 1984.

Hamilton, Alexander, James Madison and John Jay. *The Federalist Papers.* Edited by Clinton Rossiter. Signet Classic, 2003.

Harris, Robert. *Imperium.* Arrow Books, 2009.

Hawass, Zahi and Franck Goddio. *Cleopatra: The Search for the Last Queen of Egypt.* National Geographic, 2010.

Heck, J. G. *Heck's Pictorial Archive of Art and Architecture.* Dover Publications, Inc., 1994.

Heisenberg, Werner. *Physics and Philosophy.* Harper & Row, 1962.

Hughes, Robert. *Rome: A Cultural, Visual, and Personal History.* Knopf, 2011.

Humez, Alexander and Nicholas. *A B C Et Cetera: The Life & Times of the Roman Alphabet.* David R. Godine, 1985.

Huysmans, Joris-Karl, translated by Robert Baldick. *Against Nature.* Penguin, 1959.

Isaacson, Walter. "The Empire in the Mirror." *The New York Times,* May 13, 2007.

James, Simon. *Latin Matters.* Portico, 2008.

Kelman, Suanne. *All in the Family: A Cultural History of Family Life.* Viking, 1998.

Kirsch, Adam. "The Empire Strikes Back: Rome and Us." *The New Yorker,* January 9, 2012.

Koerth-Baker, Maggie. "The Mind of a Flip-Flopper." *The New York Times,* August 15, 2012.

Lecker, Robert, Jack David and Peter O'Brien. *Introduction to Literature: British, American, Canadian.* Harper & Row, 1987.

Lefkowitz, Mary R., and Maureen B. Fant. *Women in Greece and Rome.* Samuel-Stevens, 1977.

Lehrer, Jonah, "Is Google Ruining Your Memory?" "The Frontal Cortex" Wired Science blog. *Wired,* July 15, 2011.

Little, Melanie, ed. *What My Father Gave Me: Daughters Speak.* Annick Press, 2010.

Lovric, Michelle and Nikiforos Doxiadis Mardas. *How to Insult, Abuse & Insinuate in Classical Latin.* Past Times, 1998.

MacMillan, Margaret. *The Uses and Abuses of History.* Viking Canada, 2008.

Manguel, Alberto. *A History of Reading.* Viking, 1996.

Marche, Stephen. *How Shakespeare Changed Everything.* Harper Perennial, 2012.

Marshall, Amy. *Mirabilia Urbis Romae: Five Centuries of Guidebooks and Views.* University of Toronto Library, 2002.

Martin, Roger. *The Opposable Mind: How Successful Leaders Win Through Integrative Thinking.* Harvard Business School, 2007.

Martin, Sandra. *The First Man in My Life: Daughters Write About Their Fathers.* Foreword by Margaret Atwood. Penguin, 2007.

McAdam Jr., E. L., and George Milne. *Johnson's Dictionary: A Modern Selection.* Pantheon, 1962.

McCarthy, Cormac. *Blood Meridian.* Vintage, 1992.

McKeown, J. C. *A Cabinet of Roman Curiosities: Strange Tales and Surprising Facts from the World's Greatest Empire.* Oxford, 2010.

Moreno, Sylvain, et al. "Short-Term Music Training Enhances Verbal Intelligence and Executive Function," *Psychological Science,* November 2011, vol. 22 no. 11.

Morwood, James. *Pocket Oxford Latin Dictionary.* Oxford, 2005.

Mount, Harry. *Amos, Amas, Amat … And All That: How to become a Latin lover.* Short Books, 2006.

Murphy, Cullen. *Are We Rome? The Fall of an Empire and the Fate of America.* Houghton Mifflin, 2007.

Nagle, Brendan D. *The Roman World: Sources and Interpretation.* Pearson Prentice Hall, 2005.

Nielsen, Linda. *Adolescence: A Contemporary View.* Third Edition. Thomson Wadsworth, 1996.

——. *Between Fathers & Daughters.* Cumberland House, 2008.

O'Brien, Peter. "Laura Evelyn Mooney Gingras O'Brien." *The Globe and Mail,* April 24, 2002.

——. "Good, bad and Picasso." *The Toronto Star,* May 20, 2003.

——. "Economic Turmoil, Borrowed Credit, Wayward Leaders: What's New?" *COMER: The Journal of the Committee on Monetary and Economic Reform,* June 2012.

——. "Spontaneity and the single dad." *The Globe and Mail.* June 13, 2012.

OECD – Programme for International Student Assessment. "What can parents do to help their children succeed in school?" November, 2011.

Ondaatje, Michael. *Running in the Family.* McClelland and Stewart, 1982.

——. *The Story.* World Literacy of Canada / Anansi, 2004.

Orberg, Hans H. *Lingua Latina: Per se illustrate, Pars I: Familia Romana.* Focus Publishing, 2005.

Ostler, Nicholas. *Ad Infinitum: A Biography of Latin and the World It Created*. Harper Press, 2007.

——. *Empires of the Word: A Language History of the World*. HarperCollins, 2005.

Pei, Mario. *The Story of Language*. Revised Edition. J. B. Lippincott, 1965.

Plimpton, George, editor. *The Paris Review*, No. 84, Summer 1982. Interview with James Merrill by J. D. McClatchy.

Pope, Stephanie, et al. *Cambridge Latin Course, Unit 1 and Unit 2, The North American* Fourth Edition. Cambridge, 2001.

Popplewell, Brett. "Toronto revolutionary, 93, girds for one more battle," *The Toronto Star*, May 17, 2008.

Postman, Neil. *Amusing Ourselves to Death: Public Discourse in the Age of Show Business*. Penguin, 1984.

Quiller-Couch, Sir Arthur. *Studies in Literature, First Series*. Cambridge, 1930.

Raban, Jonathan. "The Getaway Car." *The New York Times Magazine*. June 12, 2011.

Ridley, Matt. *The Rational Optimist: How Prosperity Evolves*. Harper Perennial. 2010.

Rogers, Lester B., Fay Adams and Walker Brown. *The Ancient and Medieval World*. Clarke, Irwin, 1949.

Roller, Duane W. *Cleopatra: A Biography*. Oxford, 2011.

Rowland, Wade. *The Spirit of the Web: The Age of Information from Telegraph to Internet*. Somerville House, 1997.

Saylor, Steven. *Roma*. St. Martin's Griffin, 2007.

Schiff, Stacy. *Cleopatra: A Life*. Virgin, 2010.

Schuessler, Jennifer. "The Tweets of War: What's Past Is Postable." *The New York Times*, November 28, 2011.

Seabrook, John. "Streaming Dreams: YouTube Turns Pro." *The New Yorker*, January 16, 2012.

Shecter, Vicky Alvear. *Cleopatra Rules!: The Amazing Life of the Original Teen Queen*. Boyds Mills Press, 2010.

Smil, Vaclav. *Why America Is Not a New Rome*. MIT Press, 2010.

Taylor, B. C. and K. E Prentice. *Selected Latin Readings*. J. M. Dent, 1953.

Turkle, Sherry. *Alone Together: Why We Expect More from Technology and Less from Each Other*. Basic Books, 2011.

Wain, John. *Samuel Johnson: A Biography*. Viking, 1975.

Walker, Mark. *Annus Horribilus: Latin for Everyday Life.* The History Press, 2010.

Wheatley, Margaret J. *Leadership and the New Science: Discovering Order in a Chaotic World,* Third Edition. Berrett-Koehler, 2006.

Wilder, Thornton. *The Ides of March.* Grosset & Dunlap, 1950.

Young, Toby. "Forget Mandarin. Latin is the key to success." *The Spectator,* February 3, 2011.

Yourcenar, Marguerite. *Memoirs of Hadrian.* Translated by Grace Frick in collaboration with the author. Farrar, Straus and Giroux, 2005.

SELECTED ONLINE RESOURCES

www.etymonline.com
Etymology dictionary.

www.NetFamilyNews.org
A respected source of information on how the Internet is influencing and affecting our kids.

www.nodictionaries.com
A site for translating from the Latin. Enables you to insert your own text and to capture multiple meanings for each word. Great for making your own translations.

www.projectgutenberg.org
A free online source for many classical and classic authors, although often the translations are not the most compelling or recent that are available.

IMAGE CREDITS

CHAPTER INTRODUCTIONS

FILIAPATER coin: © Peter O'Brien and Lorène Bourgeois

CHAPTER 1

Feet: Illustration from *Heck's Pictorial Archive of Art and Architecture,* edited by J. G. Heck, published by Dover Publications, Inc. Copyright © 1994 Dover Publications, Inc. Reproduced with permission.
Biblia: Screen capture from Vatican.va
Vicipaedia: Courtesy of Wikipedia.org

CHAPTER 2

Humberside crest: Photograph by Peter O'Brien
Quintus: Image courtesy of Cambridge School Classics Project. Used by permission.
Hildegard: Courtesy of Wikipedia.org
Chariot Race: Photograph by Peter O'Brien and Rita Reichart
Father in Atrium: Drawing by Siobhan O'Connell
U.S. dollar: Courtesy of Wikipedia.org
Canadian coin: Courtesy of Wikipedia.org
American paper money: University of Notre Dame Rare Books & Special Collections. Used by permission.
Domitian coin: Collection of Peter O'Brien

CHAPTER 3

Memory: Courtesy of Wikipedia.org

Livi: Courtesy of Wikipedia.org
Aleppo Codex: Courtesy of Wikipedia.org
J. S. Bach: Courtesy of Wikipedia.org
Computer code: Courtesy of Arbopals Inc.
Fat naked boy: Photograph © Elizabeth Montague
Upside down boy: Photograph © David Rippner
Tabula: Courtesy of Wikipedia.org
Cosmographia: Courtesy of Wikipedia.org
Bayeux: Courtesy of Wikipedia.org

CHAPTER 4

Pompeii drawing: Courtesy of Wikipedia.org
Two Latin maps: Maps drawn by and © Peter O'Brien
Genesis: Courtesy of Wikipedia.org
SPQR: Courtesy of Wikipedia.org

CHAPTER 5

Marcus Aurelius: Photograph by Peter O'Brien
Family of characters: Drawing by Siobhan O'Connell
Picasso: Drawing by Siobhan O'Connell
Pompeii penis: Courtesy of Wikipedia.org
Two In The Trees photos: Photographs by Peter O'Brien

CHAPTER 6

Nero: Photograph by Peter O'Brien
Messalina, Agrippina and Locusta: Courtesy of Wikipedia.org
Macrobius: Courtesy of Wikipedia.org
Latin games: Courtesy of Wikipedia.org
Magazine covers: Photograph by Peter O'Brien
Mosh pit: Courtesy of Wikipedia.org

CHAPTER 7

The Ugly: Photograph by Peter O'Brien
Federalist: Courtesy of Wikipedia.org
The End: Photograph by Peter O'Brien
Cicero death: Courtesy of Wikipedia.org
Mark Antony: Courtesy of Wikipedia.org
Vitellius: Courtesy of Wikipedia.org

Sacrificed Slaves: *The Horrible History of the World.* Text copyright © Terry Deary, 2003. Illustration copyright © Martin Brown, 2003. Reproduced with the permission of Scholastic Ltd. All rights reserved.

CHAPTER 8

Rosetta: Courtesy of Wikipedia.org
Two "first computer" pics: Courtesy of Wikipedia.org

CHAPTER 9

Four Cleopatra paintings (clockwise from top left):
William Kent – © Trustees of the British Museum; Gerard Hoet – Digital image courtesy of the Getty's Open Content Program; Giambattista Tiepolo – National Gallery of Victoria. Courtesy of Wikipedia.org; Jacob Jordaens – Photograph © The State Hermitage Museum. Photo by Vladimir Terebenin, Leonard Kheifets, Yuri Molodkovets. Used by permission.
Carbonized bread: Courtesy of Wikipedia.org
Food mosaic: Courtesy of Wikipedia.org
Unswept mosaic: Courtesy of Wikipedia.org
Cleopatra coin: Courtesy of the American Numismatic Society. Used by permission.

CHAPTER 10

Tintype: Courtesy of Peter O'Brien
Every picture: Photograph by Peter O'Brien
Two faces: Two faces illustrations from *Heck's Pictorial Archive of Art and Architecture,* edited by J. G. Heck, published by Dover Publications, Inc. Copyright © 1994 Dover Publications, Inc. Reproduced with permission.
Siobhan and friends: Photograph by Peter O'Brien
Ears, eyes, mouths: From *Heck's Pictorial Archive of Art and Architecture,* edited by J. G. Heck, published by Dover Publications, Inc. Copyright © 1994 Dover Publications, Inc. Reproduced with permission.

CHAPTER 11

Caesar crossing Rubicon: Drawing by Brown Brothers, from *The Ancient and Medieval World*, by Lester B. Rogers, Fay Adams and Walker Brown.
Trajan column: Courtesy of Wikipedia.org
Oliver Goldsmith: Courtesy of Peter O'Brien

CHAPTER 12

Siobhan camping: Drawing by Siobhan O'Connell

CHAPTER 13

Latin teacher: Photograph by Peter O'Brien
Latin T-shirt: Photograph © Elana Winick
Bald ego: Photograph by Jill Standish

CHAPTER 14

Two ancient technology photographs:
Patterned Floor: Photograph © Elizabeth Montague
Roadway: Photograph © David Rippner
Ephemeris: Image from http://ephemeris.alcuinus.net/. Used by permission.
Bitcoin 1: Courtesy of Mike Caldwell. Used by permission.
Bitcoin 2 (Roman head): Courtesy of Titan Mint. Used by permission.

CHAPTER 15

Dear Daddy: Drawing by Siobhan O'Connell
Book of Kells: Courtesy of Wikipedia.org
Shaking hands 1: Photograph © David Rippner
Shaking hands 2: Courtesy of Peter O'Brien
Shaking hands 3: Photograph by Peter O'Brien

Images used as graphics in text boxes come from *Heck's Pictorial Archive of Art and Architecture* and are used by permission. All other unspecified images and graphics are courtesy of Peter O'Brien.

Every effort has been made to trace and contact copyright holders of all graphic material. Where the attempt has been unsuccessful, the publishers would be pleased to rectify any omissions.

TEXT CREDITS

Portions of this book have appeared previously in print – sometimes in slightly different form – in *Argyle, The Globe and Mail, The Toronto Star,* and *Comer: The Journal of the Committee on Monetary and Economic Reform.*

INDEX